# Contents

## About the Author

For Sharon, life with God, centered in God, is full of purpose and meaning. She is a survivor of many of life's tragedies. As a young mother she stood beside the graveside of two small sons and asked every imaginable question. These were things one read about in the newspaper that happened to *other* people. It was heartbreaking to bury her children. It changed her forever. Sharon needed different answers than the ones she was hearing from well-intentioned people. She could <u>not</u> believe "It was God's will" that children are crushed in cars so God can have children in his flower garden. She needed them in her flower garden. What kind of God hurls cars into bridges in order to snatch children for his garden? Not her God!

The author went on her own spiritual quest that lasted several years. She faithfully attended a Bible study. She asked <u>all</u> of her questions. She found different answers. She invites you to listen in and learn from her quest. She invites you to have the courage to begin and pursue daily your own spiritual quest for an active dynamic faith in God.

Sharon began her professional training for ministry in her forties. She holds degrees in Psychology, Religion, Philosophy and also a Master of Divinity Degree. She has served churches in suburban, rural, and inner-city areas. She produced a meditation video "Holy Moments." She designed and teaches an inner awareness class: "Staying Right-Side-Up in a Topsy-Turvy World." While Sharon was on leave of absence writing this book, she worked for the Roman Catholic Church managing the largest food pantry in Springfield, Illinois, the state capitol. She volunteered at St. John's Breadline, which serves 550 meals a day to the homeless and underprivileged. Sharon feels blessed by both Protestants and Roman Catholics. Her co-workers were of endless inspiration during the writing, polishing, and creative process of *Stand With Angels*.

# Acknowledgement

Writing a book is like creating a fine work of art from a chunk of marble. You chisel a little here, chip a little there. My first readers were faithful even though what they were reading was far removed from the end product. I am amazed they could see a book emerging from this chunk of stone. Each suggestion helped me chisel and chip away at what it was I believed God wanted it to be. This book is the creation of hundreds of people.

**I am extremely grateful** for the remarks of: Shirley Davidson, Betty Frobish, Art Heemer, Roy Nash, Alice Ramey and her mother Gladys, Patt and Michael Sheahan. GayeEllen Kick was the patient proof-reader *par excellence*. Beth McQuade added skilled objectivity. Tony Sanquedolce, my graphc artist, added his insightful touch of beauty and mystique to the cover, photos and text. I am grateful for the comments of Barbara Gurtler, my mountain-climbing friend. *This* adventure was one mountain I never expected to climb. I am grateful for those who read and believed in me as an author before I did.

**I was inspired** by the photography of T.J. Salzman and Kathy Krstulovich. I was encouraged by Patty Johansen. I treasured the comments of Rosie Voyles. I was urged onward by former professors Dr. Robert Tuttle and Dr. Ruth Duck with editing suggestions. My former District Superintendent, Mary Vick Roth, offered invaluable suggestions. My former parishioners, Becky Collins and Pat Grizzard, always gave me the encouragement I needed whenever I needed it. John and Luella Lenwell shed tears of understanding; they read and comprehended far too much. And thank you, Bill Day, for the invitation to speak at the Full Gospel Business Men's Fellowship. Sharing the miracles that day was a turning point for me. I needed to tell the story! Who could fail with all of this support?

I have one regret. When the "Defense Fund" was set up at Bank One, I was still in a state of shock and I did not request a list of donors. Without a list, I was unable to thank those who contributed. Whoever you are—God bless you and know that your giving did make a difference. Without your help, it is possible this book would not be in your hands.

## Warning—Disclaimer

This book is a 31-day devotional based on a true story. It is of a Judeo-Christian orientation theologically, although the author is both open and accepting of the truths about the Divine that can be found in other theological traditions. Within the book are exercises the reader can use to enhance perceptions of the Divine interacting with the reader through Scripture, prayer, journalizing, reflection, meditation, music, scenery, art, and other similar media. In short, this book is designed to enhance one's spiritual journey through life—finding the Divine in the moment and in the midst of personal pain and crisis.

The author makes no claims of either spiritual or psychological expertise, other than the spiritual and psychological truths she has found along her spiritual life's journey. In fact, your use of this book in your daily devotional life will probably cause truth and interaction with the Divine to unfold in a richly different way than has the author's interaction with the Divine.

Every effort has been made to make this publication accurate and to acknowledge the contributions of other's intellectual property. However, there may be mistakes, both typographical and/or in content. Should you find one, please feel free to contact the publisher at the address found in the book and a correction will certainly appear in the next edition.

The purpose of this book is to educate and enrich. The author and Angel Writing Mill shall have neither liability nor responsibility to any person or entity with respect to any loss or damage caused, or alleged to be caused, directly or indirectly by the information contained in this book.

**Should you not wish to be bound by the above, you may return this book
to the publisher in undamaged condition for a full refund.**

# STAND WITH ANGELS

## Conversations With God From The Eye Of The Storm

This 31-day spiritual quest is dedicated to *you* as you seek a closer walk with God. It is my prayer you will find hope and encouragement through your own quest for meaning. Upon reflection, I am amazed at the degree of peace and the presence of God I discovered *in* the wilderness.

God was there.
God spoke ever so softly:

*Your answer will come,*
*But not as you expect.*

## ONE BEGINNING

When my children were tots, they played with a tot-sized inflatable toy. Fading memory tells me the toy had a sand base and was made in the image of a bear or clown. When the kids punched it, the toy leaned all the way down to the floor… and popped right back up. PUNCH! Down it went… and back up. PUNCH! Down… Up. It was fun… for the kids.

During the years when I was writing this book, I often felt like that punch toy. PUNCH! Down I go... and right back up. PUNCH! Down. Up. My spiritual and emotional life imitated the up-down-up motion of the punching toy. It wasn't fun.

During these years, basically I learned FOUR THINGS. First, I learned to rely on a different method of prayer, which I will share later.

Second, I learned about inner city ministry. I was the pastor of an inner city church. It was a very different experience from suburban or rural ministry. Crisis situations were the norm of every day.

Third, I learned to reflect on what it means to be related to someone who was incarcerated. I was in a situation in which someone I loved was in prison. Coming from a white middle-class background, this was something I never thought would touch my life.

Fourth, I learned with a new depth of certainty that God is present at all times. I am a person who experiences the usual ups and downs of life. However, from the experiences in inner city ministry and the incarcerated, I learned *God is with us* <u>especially</u> in the down times! *God is with us*, appearing in diverse loving ways, at <u>all</u> times! Like St. Paul in Romans 8:38 and 39, "I am convinced… NOTHING can separate us from the love of God…." [*my condensed version*]

In all these circumstances, I experienced God's presence as never before. I experienced God's presence in persons and in places I never expected to see God. Surprises included finding God in my inner city neighbors (who were <u>not</u> considered model citizens by some), finding God in prison in a gang leader, and finding God in angels who appeared both in human form and in the supernatural.

Throughout these years, God allowed me the freedom to struggle. I learned from struggling to make different choices <u>or</u> never to do *that* again as I regrouped. I learned to ask God different questions. Less and less, I asked, "Why God? Why me?" More often, I asked, "What am I learning from this person or this situation?" Less and less, I asked, "God, how can I trust so-and-so?" More and more, I asked, "God, given my history and experience, how and who can I learn to trust?" Sometimes I asked, "God, could you show me those persons who have earned the right to be trusted?" It was liberating to be totally honest with God, to ask new questions, to ask <u>all</u> my questions—NO HOLDING BACK! I found freedom in the struggle.

This freedom can be yours, too, if you also feel like that punch toy. In **Stand With Angels**, I am sharing a method that helped me experience this new freedom. Everybody's spirituality and life experiences are different, but I offer mine to you. The method I offer you is written prayer. I began writing down my thoughts 15 or 20 years ago to "Dear God…" and signed off with "Love, Sharon." Over the years, I sporadically continued writing in notebooks (later called journals). During the years I was in inner city ministry, I wrote a monthly newsletter column for my parish—"Conversations With God." The column was written to inspire *hope* for hundreds of readers as well as for me. I needed hope. These conversations with God became dialogues in prayer. The 31 action reflection meditations in this book evolved from those written prayers. I invite you to listen in, contemplate, and respond.

Each article tells a small part of the story. There was a great deal going on *behind* the scene. It was what was happening *behind* the scene that drove me to wrestle with God, drove me to seek God *in* the wilderness. Although the readers were unaware of my personal struggles, they reported being inspired by the articles. It was not the time to share my personal struggles.

The structure of this book tells some of the background, the storms, and the blessings. I offer suggestions to help you create your own personal journal. I offer reasons why you do not want to procrastinate.

Just do it now! Then, you will encounter 31 conversations with God followed by action reflection questions for your personal meditation time. In the photo section at the back of the book are samples of what helps me focus on the Divine. More will be said of this later. Read the meditation, ponder the questions, reflect on the photos if so desired, and begin your own freedom struggle. You may need to read through each conversation more than once. Read slowly, read aloud. Picture what is happening in your mind. Does anything relate to you? I encourage you to adapt whatever process works for you. I will say more about this later. Following the 31 action reflection meditations, I share how endings can become beginnings. The epilogue, ONE ENDING—ANOTHER BEGINNING, tells more of what was going on behind the scenes, more of what I literally experienced as miracles. I could not explain the angels. They appeared. That is the only way I can explain it.

And now, I return to my first image. What about the inflatable punching toy? Actually, if I remember correctly, the toy was larger than the tot. Problems usually seem larger at first to me. Regardless of the size of the problem or the punching toy, have you been there? Are you there now? If so, I will wager you don't enjoy being there. In fact, the up-down experience drains away energy and joy. Enough is enough! It is easy to have *faith* in God when things are going well in our lives. How-ever, as author Rabbi Harold S. Kushner and many of us know, bad things <u>do</u> happen even to good people. Life isn't fair. How do you hold onto your *faith* when life appears to be falling apart?

Having said that, we know life often resembles that of the inflatable punching toy. Some of us get punched one too many times. Do you know someone who feels defeated in spirit, mind, and body? Are you that person? As I said, enough is enough! Step out of the punching zone. Step into the presence of God. How? Let's explore together. It took time for me to learn the process. I am a slow learner! I learned to step into the presence of God from the eye of the storm. God did not take away the storm. And trite as it may sound, I did not go through the storm alone. I learned to practice the presence of God wherever I needed to do so. It became *my choice* to focus on the Divine rather than to take a spiritual and emotional beating.

This book was birthed to help people hold on to faith during hard times at all times. It needs to be pondered, savored, and shared. As you read it, first read it for yourself. Watch for the angels and know that you, too, *Stand With Angels*.

## BACKGROUND HISTORY

The first readers of these meditations were part of the inner city ministries of a small church in the state capitol of Springfield, Illinois. Some were volunteers of the Children's Supper Hour, an after-school program, in progress for over a decade. Some were part of the Shalom Zone movement launched early in 1994. Some helped renovate the former church parsonage into a People Empowerment Center. The center evolved as a result of Shalom training and from needs in the neighborhood.

At one time, the residential area around the church of 500 members was very quiet. Over the past 30 years, the congregation gradually diminished to fewer than 100 members. White, middle-class members moved away to other parts of the city. A remnant returned faithfully to worship in an area that had painfully changed from bliss to violence. Bloodshed and crime were steadily increasing.

It was not uncommon to read in the newspaper "Police Beat" reports of crime in our neighborhood. Numerous times the church properties and the surrounding area were featured on the front page. There were articles on stabbings, robberies, drive-by shootings, and drug busts. It was not uncommon to hear police sirens at any time of day or night. It was not uncommon to find police cars in the church parking lot. One evening, I counted seven police cars and a police dog responding to a reported burglary at the house next door to the church. The same evening, members of the men's group and the women's group were holding their monthly meeting. Most of the men and women were over 65; several were in their 80's. Not unlike the early disciples, they met behind locked doors.

Little did I know what I was getting into! Concern for personal safety was now a necessity. Violence became my next door neighbor! Within days after I arrived in the parish, I was given a pepper gas vial to attach to my keys; this was always clipped to my belt. The pepper gas was of no use to me in a purse, briefcase, or desk drawer. Fortunately, I only needed to use it once during an incident of domestic violence next door to the church. I ended up between a man who had blackened the eye and beat up a woman from the parish. Her frightened children ran next door to Grandma's house. Before the police arrived, I stood on the front stoop with pepper gas in hand saying to the young man, "You are not coming in here!" He didn't.

My parish was one of two congregations that birthed the first Shalom Zone in central and southern Illinois. In case you are unfamiliar with Shalom Zones, the Shalom concept of holistic renewal grew out of the denomination's response to the 1992 Los Angeles riots after the Rodney King verdict. The Hebrew word, SHALOM, means more than an absence of conflict. It means God's wholeness in every aspect of life—spiritually, socially, relationally, educationally, and economically. One of the riches I discovered was God's wholeness creates tranquility in the soul, even in the midst of life's storms.

Two congregations, one predominantly Black and one predominantly White (mine), designated 70 square blocks between the two churches as their declared SHALOM ZONE. Although the two congregations had had racial difficulties in the past, they formed a covenant to work together in transforming a decaying area into God's wholeness. This was not an easy task; it was not a simple task. The problems were complex and deeply rooted. Many times we took two steps backward and one step forward. However, you will notice in "Conversations With God," that it was in celebrating the small successes that long-range goals were accomplished. Two pastors, one a black man, the other a white woman (myself), led our congregations carefully around racial land mines and obstacles in order to turn a war zone into a place of peace and mutual respect.

It was a challenge serving God in the inner city. Vividly imprinted on my mind was the Friday afternoon I confronted one of our "neighbors." It was a beautiful summer day. On my way to make a prison visit, I drove by the church and *there he was again!* I had asked residents in the neighborhood about the man who made it his habit to dwell in his car right next to the church. "Oh, he's a local drug dealer." When I appealed to the police, they said there was nothing they could do. Technically he was not breaking the law, and he was on public property.

However, I knew the children passed by him on their way to the after-school program—Children's Supper Hour/KIDSPACE. I decided that if I could prevent it, he was not going to entice these children into drugs. After parking my car across the street, I reached under the seat for my camera. I made an attempt to be nonchalant as I walked behind his car and around to the front passenger seat where he was sitting with the car door open. I snapped his picture. He said, "What are you doing?" I responded, "I want you out of here!" No longer was he seen parked at his usual site.

There were painful transitions in the children's program as we moved from merely providing a meal to creating safe space and building relationships with the children. Some of the elderly volunteers did not have the patience needed to work with the children. There were times I did not have the patience! The children and their families were surrounded by so much violence. It accompanied them wherever they went. Sometimes I would go home… and weep

Always, I wrestled with what needed to be done to make a difference in the neighborhood. I had inherited, from the former pastor, the concept of KIDSPACE in the supper program. KIDSPACE was designed to build relationships by spending quality time with the children. KIDSPACE was an alternative to the violent environment outside. It was designed to keep the kids off the streets a little longer. Not every volunteer who served the supper hour appreciated this new concept.

There were three incidents I remember vividly that made me a believer in the concept of KIDSPACE. One was the day I heard police and ambulance sirens just outside the backdoor of the church. A child was lying in the street. A little boy had been struck down by a car. The driver drove away and disappeared. Another was the day I discovered a five-year-old boy sitting in the back seat of a police car. The boy had broken a basement window in the church. Someone in the neighborhood had called the police. Interceding, I took the boy and his mother inside; I showed them the sanctuary. We knelt at the altar for prayer, and they went home. Another incident involved one of three brothers, ages eleven, nine, and eight, who had minimal supervision. Their parents had a reputation for being on drugs. The boys were often seen on the street without coats and mittens in frigid weather. A police car was parked in the church parking lot. In the back seat was the youngest boy, picked up for carrying drugs. For me, the original plan—feed the children supper and send them home—was not enough! In the ten years the program had been in progress, the neighborhood environment had drastically changed. It was no longer a quiet place to live. One needed to survive!

"Conversations With God" helped me deal with attitudes, obstacles, and transitions. This was not an easy place to serve God. Never in my wildest dreams did I imagine serving in the inner city. I was a "country girl." Well, this country girl fell in love with the kids, the families. There is a saying, "You can take the girl out of the country, but you can't take the *country* out of the girl." You can also take the pastor out of the Shalom Zone, but you can't take the *Shalom* out of the pastor! Shalom, God's holistic peace helps you survive any storm. Once you find shalom, it is always with you and you never want to let it go!

*God gave me a gift* by placing me in the inner city. God did not remove all the obstacles or the dangers. My greatest gift… was growing closer to God. *God's presence was there.* You will notice in my first "Conversation With God" that I was very excited about serving as pastor of this church. As I walked in the neighborhood, I learned and I grew. As I walked beside some of the older members of the congregation, I was touched by the hopelessness, the unwillingness to "try again" to revitalize their church in the inner city. To be in the inner city, where there are many injustices daily, was truly where I needed to be. I learned of courage and justice when I needed courage and release from injustice. On this journey, I gained precious insights and spiritual depth. These are blessings! I was blessed! Very soon, I would need blessings. The storms were about to hit!

*God gave me another gift.* Ten years ago I prayed, "God, if I am to marry, you select my husband." After being married 25 years and single for ten, I was surprised when God dropped a wonderful man into my life. Now that is Amazing Grace! We were good friends. We were both surprised when we realized God had another idea: MARRIAGE—soul mates and partners in life! He was not the man I expected; I was not the woman he expected! With plans of marriage in our future, we requested parishes no further than 50 miles apart. We were appointed to serve parishes over 120 miles apart (Oh, boy!). His parish was in the heart of farmland; my parish was in the inner city as described. As we served, we were deluged by storm after storm of trials and tribulations. Some of these trials were plain old evil. There were times we felt abandoned by our peers, as well as by the church hierarchy. We found ourselves in a wilderness. What is a wilderness? I think of a wilderness as a strange land or place I really don't want to be—a barren place, a place of hardship, a place void of joy or peace, a place of misery, an abyss.

This was not my first journey through a wilderness. I remember another wilderness (years ago) in which I discovered angel visits came in threes. At least, it took three visits for me to realize the angels were at it again! The angels were ministering to me as they ministered to Jesus in his wilderness experience in Matthew 4:11 and Mark 1:13. Check it out!

Through four decades of life, I rarely thought about angels prior to the angel visits in threes. The only memory I had of angels was when I was six years old. I stood on the far side of the room and watched as my grandfather was dying. I remember someone said, "I saw two angels behind him." I didn't see the angels.

There are many things we do not see and yet we can still have faith in God. In the Old Testament, I have often wondered how Joseph, who had the Coat of Many Colors, kept his faith. His brothers literally left him in a pit to die. Then they couldn't live with themselves so they pulled him out and sold him into slavery. Later, after surviving those atrocities, he was falsely accused of rape by Potiphar's wife and spent years in prison. Also in the Old Testament, Daniel was carried off into exile. Daniel was living a wilderness experience in a strange land under miserable circumstances. Where was God? Reading the New Testament, I have often wondered how the disciples held on to their faith when they were persecuted? Their existence was one crisis after another. Steven was stoned to death. Paul and Peter were both arrested and put in jail. How did they hang onto their faith? I pondered these things.

Today, we still have crises and wilderness experiences. We can learn from each other. We can learn from the ancient masters. We can learn to read between the lines of the biblical pages. One of the purposes of this book is to practice reading between the lines with the help of the Holy Spirit. God's

Holy Spirit is very much alive!

Let's talk about crises. There are many types of crises. Perhaps your crisis is *physical*—threat of bodily harm, disease, impairment, or the reality of the aging process. Perhaps it is *relational*—wounds caused by childhood abuse, infidelity, divorce, death of a spouse or a child. Perhaps it is *financial*—threat (or reality) of job loss, eviction, bankruptcy. Maybe you have banged your head against a wall and have not been able to get a job. Maybe your skills aren't what are needed; you need training. Perhaps it is a *social* crisis. You don't seem to fit in. You moved away from family and friends. You have not made new friends. You have no support structure. You feel alone! All of these crises take a toll on emotions. Often you need someone to talk to, an unbiased sounding board, or a professional counselor. Sometimes a prescription for an anti-depressant is needed to chemically balance a person to the point where he/she can deal with life. Pulling out of depression is often not something that can be done without help. Please hear me: This book will not, cannot, do it all! The whole person is affected by crises. Get the help you need.

Your crisis may be a mixture of several of the above or all of the above and then some! Often during these times, we do not sense God's presence with us. I call these times… a wilderness. The rules of life, or what was presumed to be the rules of life, have run amuck. We thought we were living right, serving God as best we knew how; it did not seem to matter. As the bumper sticker flashes at us—**STUFF HAPPENS!** [*Sharon's version*] Don't give up! Let's explore the wilderness together!

## STORMS

Let me repeat. Two congregations were building SHALOM in the inner city. Over 120 miles apart, two pastors were serving God, falling in love, and planning a marriage. The storms hit and we were riding it out. During this time, I discovered the *eye of the storm*—that sacred tranquil place where nothing can touch you. I call this sacred space—SHALOM, God's Wholeness.

In the heat of the summer, SIMULTANEOUS STORMS struck both of us… the very same day! Most pastors do not expect their church will be robbed and vandalized. All of the frozen meat (a freezer full at the time) was carried away into the night. This meat was used to feed the children of the neighborhood! How dare anyone take food meant for the children! The window and frame were destroyed. Shards of glass were scattered atop canned goods and boxes of macaroni; it was all a mess on the floor. The church leaders and I felt violated. Angry!

The phone rang. It just happened to be… the other Shalom pastor who did not yet know of the break-in. Over the phone line, he prayed for us. He sent two men over to help clean up the mess. I call them angels. How we appreciated those two African American angels ministering to a "White" church. It was a long day! It became even longer!

Home at last, I checked the phone messages. One hundred twenty miles away, my fiancé's voice stunned my ears, "The police are on their way to arrest me. Get hold of someone. Let someone know what is happening! I need to arrange bail." Another storm! By the time I called back, there was no answer. Falsely accused, he was arrested. The police took him away, handcuffed, in the back seat of a police car. In a matter of hours, we went from faithfully serving God to wondering what had hit us. We felt totally alone, abandoned, vulnerable, facing the unknown, out there.

During these storms, I wrote "Conversation With God # 3." It was amazing! God was ministering to me through my own writing, my own article. I needed to hang on to my faith and take it one step at a time! I needed to seek God's guidance and see myself as an inspiration to others. This was not a time to give up on hope, to give up on God!

Over the next three years, we experienced the emotional and spiritual roller coaster ride of the legal system. We learned not every American can afford the high fees of a good attorney. We learned… not everyone wins their case! To make a long story short, my fiancé served 21 months in prison as a result of an angry person lashing out with a false accusation. The exoneration process would take years! It was a devastating experience for both of us. For him, what appeared to be the loss of his ministry and his honor was a tremendous loss. For myself, it was painful to stand by helpless and watch his life shredded. This was America! This did not happen in America! Where was the God of truth and justice? What was happening in a legal system which did not appear to be just? How could a state's attorney blatantly get away with tainting the only witness? We discovered we had no weapons to fight this, and we definitely did not have enough money!

We also learned in a case of false accusation, the accused has the task of putting the puzzle pieces together in the dark. Actually, the accused is not even given all the pieces. Many pieces were unknown to us until after the trial, sentencing, and incarceration. It was then that I demanded from our attorney every piece of paper connected with the case. After studying the documents in consultation with a forensic expert, we came to believe our attorney (without our permission or knowledge) had worked out a bargain with the state's attorney when the money ran out. Maybe our attorney simply believed the accusation was true. We may never know. He is no longer our attorney.

I woke up to a different view of America. Here I stood ministering to people who carried the pain and wounds of injustice, while I carried my own personal pain of injustice inflicted upon someone I loved. *If you really want to hurt me, hurt someone I love!* During these three years in inner city ministry, I could personally identify with the injustice in the parish and in the neighborhood. As I carved out niches of peace through my journal notes to God, my faith and spirituality grew.

I grew spiritually through the period of incarceration. Being white, middle-class, I never thought I would be visiting someone in prison. Every week, I drove two hours to a medium/max prison to visit the man I will refer to as Daniel. From a Christian inmate, we learned in Hebrew, Daniel means "God is my judge." We had trusted the "unjust judge." Now, all we had to trust in was God. I was searched each time. Daniel was strip-searched. We met in the visiting room with scores of other inmates and visitors. Sitting at a three-foot square dining table, we prayed, "God, please give us some hope. Please don't be… so silent." Month after month, I spent hours waiting for Daniel to join me in the visitor's room. As I waited, I prayed for God's presence to surround the guards as well as the inmates.

## BLESSINGS

New perceptions came to me that I had never before imagined. Like Jesus, my friend and fiancé was a convicted criminal. I was in love with <u>two</u> convicted criminals; both men were falsely accused. Jesus went before an unjust judge, a man who chose to wash his hands of the whole business rather than take a stand for justice. Jesus was never exonerated in any court of law. I began to understand angels surrounded Jesus in the Garden of Gethsemane. Those angels surely did not abandon him during his beating, trial, or while dying on the cross. I did not notice the angels surrounding us until later.

Months passed before I saw evidence of God's presence in prison. I witnessed many miracles, and an Epiphany that I will share later. There were visits from supernatural angels and angels in human bodies. I would not trade those blessings for anything. Nor would I ever want to go through something like this again. There were many tears, a great deal of despair, and yet, *God was there*. My perception changed. Also, I came to understand that blessings come in waves. More about waves later!

Well into the second year of this journey, a friend gave me a vivid image of hope. Alice had been my counseling elder during my professional training in the process for ordained ministry. She knew Daniel and I were feeling abandoned by our peers and by God. Alice said to me:

Do you remember little Jessica, the 18-month-old baby, who fell down a narrow well? For days, people were glued to their television sets, praying, and hoping rescue workers would reach her in time. Little Jessica had no way of knowing what was going on above her. She was down in the well. There was *no* way she could comprehend the flurry of loving activity going on above her on her behalf. I can only believe a whole lot is going on that we can't see.

The LITTLE JESSICA IMAGE, a true story that happened years ago in October of 1987, sustained my faith when nothing else could.

## ENDINGS AND BEGINNINGS

As I let go of my personal storms and crises, I *knew* others shared similar and worse experiences. Yet, I had questions! How <u>do</u> you get through difficult times? How do you keep from losing your faith when you don't see God? You don't need books like this when you are having marvelous spiritual highs. Before I go any further, I want to explain more about my writing to God and how over time it evolved into <u>God responding</u> to my notes. What began as a monologue, shifted to dialogue. I was surprised to discover God could write back to me through my own pen. It was 15 or 20 years ago that I began writing. I poured out my thoughts and questions onto paper addressed "Dear God" and signed "Love, Sharon." In the past couple of years, I began to put my pen down and wait a few moments. Then, I picked the pen back up and began to write again. This time I wrote "Dear Sharon" and signed "Love, God." While admitting my own human imperfection and realizing it would be easy to stray from a Divine message, I was <u>amazed</u> at the insights that poured out onto the paper. I am not claiming infallible Divine inspiration. I only know that new and helpful insights were surfacing in written form on my journal pages. I repeat, I am not claiming infallible Divine inspiration. I believe no mortal human being has the whole truth or revelation of God. Humans are only capable of receiving bits and fragments of the Divine.

Before the dialogue I refer to could happen, I had to find some *quiet space with God* in my day. Many times it was during breakfast, which was eaten in solitude before my daily work routine. Most of the time it was at my kitchen table. During mild weather, I would sit at the patio table on my deck overlooking a small pond. In other words, I had to find a place, a space, where God and I would not be interrupted for the next 10, 20, or 30 minutes. The radio and television were turned off. The only sounds I wanted to hear were birds and crickets. A gentle breeze on my face helped me to relax as I soaked in the presence of God… and wrote. Sometimes, I would read a Bible passage first, sometimes not. It was a quiet, private, honest time spent just between God and me. During the storms I needed God most.

I practiced a reflective time each day through doing theology at sunset. Simply, daily, I asked myself, "Where was God today?" The beauty of the sunset helped me focus on the good and wonderful events of the day. Even on the rainiest day, I was reminded somewhere… there was a beautiful sunset. Regardless of the pain, I believe God is GOOD and wonderful! I believe God is active in all of life, in the inner city and even in prison. I practiced being *still* and finding God.

I needed a way of staying focused on God, of *being with God.* SO MANY mundane distractions were <u>all</u> competing for my attention! For example, the refrigerator was running. The air conditioner (or furnace) kicked on. The lights buzzed softly. Outside, I could hear cars and trucks on the highway. I could hear hammers from a construction site; an airplane flew over head. I could hear kids rough-housing at the pond, a baby crying. Whenever I sought out my quiet time with God, NOISE interrupted. I needed to focus! Lighting a candle and playing soft music helped me to focus. I needed to tune out distractions in order to tune in to God's harmony. It has been said that Dwight L. Moody believed, "If you can get an unsaved person to be quiet for five minutes and to think on Eternity, he/she can be saved without speaking a word of the Gospel." Simply put: *Be still and know God.* It sounds easy, but in our continual flood of sound, it is <u>not</u> easy.

Then there were the visual distractions! There were butterflies, mosquitoes, birds flying, clouds, people jogging by, bunnies scampering, ducks landing on the pond. Focus, Sharon, FOCUS! Putting a pen in my hand, touching it to the paper—writing a word, a phrase, a sentence—helped me focus. Eventually, I found it helpful to write down my thoughts in a journal. You may or may not find this helpful. I found I would easily forget what I had prayed for, or what concerns I'd had. Reflections upon these entries helped build my faith and made me stronger as I recognized answers to prayer. Looking back in my journal, I saw where I had actually pleaded with God, "Send your angels!" Yet, I was surprised when angels appeared. I was surprised at the way God revealed the angels to me. Writing and reflection became exercises in building spiritual muscle. These were times of *knowing.* I *knew* God was there. I didn't need neon lights. I just *knew*!

Whatever time or place you seek to converse with God will become sacred. Where might you find your niche of time and space? I lived alone, which made it easier. However, I began writing to God when my children were still at home. I would write in the middle of the night if I could not sleep. Often I wrote early in the morning before anyone else was awake. Perhaps for you it could be a quiet solitary lunch at a picnic table in the park, or in a solarium or atrium. Learn to tune out others by placing your back toward distractions, by focusing on blue sky or a beautiful landscape. Perhaps there is an intriguing work of art near you on which to focus.

The photo section in the back of this book helps me focus on the Divine. When I take a few moments to look away from my problems to look at images that remind of what is good and Holy, I find it easier to focus. These photos have personal meaning for me. One is of my seminary. Another was a sunset taken from the Shrine of St. Therese in Juneau, Alaska. I stayed in the lodge at St. Therese while on a Volunteer In Mission trip. Another is a Canadian sunset over tranquil waters. The last is a recent photo of my grandchild. I change the photos I carry as I collect new ones that inspire me. Be on the lookout for inspiring scenes in magazines, photos, or in works of art.

Beauty helps me focus on God. Where is your place of beauty? Is it near your sleeping child? Is it in your quiet office before the workday begins, at your kitchen table, in the bedroom, or in the den? Find your space and time. Give God a chance to write to you. Give God the opportunity to move you from monologue to dialogue.

Use this book however it works best for you. You may study it over a one-month period by reflecting and writing your responses to the questions by filling in the blanks. You might study it once each season or once a year. Some pages will speak to you. Others won't. Move on! This is simply a tool for you to use on your unique spiritual walk with God.

Please do not procrastinate. One of my friends and spiritual mentors is 75. She is a beautiful person inside and out. She shared with me, "I wish I had learned the habit of meditation on paper as you have." Like many of us, she asks the deeper questions, "How do I grow old gracefully? How do I face death?

How do I face life in a deteriorating body?" It is never too late to start. Grab a scrap of paper, date it, write on it, and throw it in a file. In a month or so, tape the pieces in a notebook or scrapbook. DO IT NOW—was the motto we used when I sold skin-care for Mary Kay Cosmetics in the early '80s. Be a member of the DIN DIN CLUB! **Do It** Now! The greatest obstacle to getting started is writing the <u>first</u> word!

Today is the ONLY day we have. Tomorrow is ALWAYS tomorrow. If I wait for the perfect moment to jot down my thoughts and questions to God, it will NEVER come. If I wait for my writing skills to improve without actually practicing writing, it won't happen. God isn't impressed with good grammar. Just BE an honest, sincere seeker.

If you absolutely cannot write due to paralysis or a disability, an alternative suggestion to journaling is to use a tape recorder. As you speak into the recorder, state the date and time each time you record. Example: "January 2, 1999, Saturday 2:30 p.m. I have some questions for you, God. These are my thoughts and my questions…."

This is what I used to do when I first started. Don't laugh! Each year when my daughters got out of school, I saved their old notebooks. I tore out the used pages and used the rest for my "notes to God." The covers always had their names and doodling on the front. I found magazine pictures I liked and taped my pictures over the cover. It was now MINE. My first journal cover had a woodsy scene with a stream meandering over rocks and tree roots. That scene was tranquilizing to my soul. On your spiritual quest, think about what you like and need. When thumbing through magazines, if a scene or scenario grabs you, it just might be an important link between you and the Divine.

If you are not as frugal as I, just buy a notebook or a journal. Take a marker and print "For My Eyes Only" on the front and back cover. Place a sturdy rubber band around your notebook. WHY? As you are pouring out your intimate thoughts on paper, you don't want others to read it <u>unless</u> you give them permission. This allows you freedom to be totally honest with God <u>and</u> to have confidentiality. There may be times you will want to share a portion, a page, or a paragraph with someone else. Caution! Be selective! This is your sacred ground. Be careful not to leave your notebook out where others might see it and read it. If you want to write in strict confidence, you may <u>not</u> want to write in this book. It is your book and your choice.

Have fun with your journal—use colored ink pens/pencils, draw smiley faces, etc. *LIGHTEN UP!* Let your spirit play. Be gentle with yourself. You may miss a day (or a week, or a month) of writing. Begin again; go on. Give yourself permission to be messy! Nowhere does it say a journal must be neat! It is okay to use sentence fragments. You may not even write a whole paragraph. Then again, you may find yourself writing page after page. Each person is at a different place. You may not be able to write a word at this time, but you may pick it up and write a month or a year from now. There are no exams, no grades, no neatness tests!

Your time with your journal is a time to honestly let your thoughts flow to God on paper. When scriptures or quotations come to mind, jot them down. When new thoughts come to mind, jot them down. ALWAYS label any entry with the time of day, the day, and date. You will appreciate this later during reflection. God bless you on your quest!

Sharon Colbért

# CONVERSATION WITH GOD
## # 1

Dear GOD,

This is my first newsletter to the folks in my new parish.  What on earth do I write?  Do I dare tell them <u>how</u> <u>excited</u> I am to be their pastor?  Do I dare tell them <u>how</u> <u>excited</u> I am about their faithfulness, their love of peppy music, their ministry to the children?  YOU know these are my first loves.  Right after Jesus, I love music, people, prayer, serving you, but not always in that order.

GOD, people have asked me where I will be serving.  I tell them.  They say, "I <u>don't</u> <u>know</u> that church."  I tell them, "This is the church whose Shalom Zone march was featured on the televised news!"  They say, "OH!"  (I smile with pride.  I am so proud of their decision to become a Shalom Zone!)

They say, "Where <u>is</u> it?"  I say, "It is on the corner of 13th and South Grand."  They say, "Your church is <u>there</u>?"  I say, "Yes, we are the church with the latch-key ministry to children!"  (I smile with pride again.)

They say, "You are going to live <u>there</u>?"  I say, "Not exactly.  I am not far away.  I am going to <u>walk</u> <u>there</u> (I have already taken my first walk), and <u>talk</u> <u>there</u> with folks, and help discover YOUR presence <u>there</u>!"

GOD, why do people have so much difficulty believing you care about them, believing in your presence on 13th and South Grand?  Is anything too hard for you?

## *I didn't think so!*

*I know… that I know… that I know…* you are there.  Lead us, God!  Help us "be as wise as serpents and as innocent as doves."  [*Matthew 10:16 NRSV*]  Help us get to know one another, build trust, and fellowship together. Let those who need to be refreshed in you feel the gentle breeze of your Holy Spirit on their brow. Let those who are wounded find healing. Let those who grieve shed their tears and someday know joy. Let those who do not yet see Jesus, <u>see</u> Jesus.

> We cannot <u>know</u> him without <u>seeing</u> him.
> We cannot <u>love</u> him without <u>knowing</u> him.
> We cannot <u>serve</u> him without <u>loving</u> him. [*Holy Land Lecture, Dr. Charles Page*]

OKAY, GOD, we are counting on you to nudge, guide, and support us. We need you.

In Joy and In Peace,

*Sharon*


## ACTION REFLECTION:

Wherever **this type face** appears, the assertion is that God has answered in some way. In other words, the assertion is that **nothing is too hard for God.** God cares for persons in the inner city where violence is a daily occurrence. Claiming God as your guide—who does indeed care for us— ponder the following questions as they apply to your life. First, tune out distractions as much as possible. Turn off the phone, radio, etc. Pick up pen or pencil and write a sentence, a paragraph, or a full page. What is in your heart and on your mind? Be honest with God. Nothing is too large, too complicated, or too difficult to be shared with God. Clear your head of worries by putting the problems and worries down on paper. This tacks down the worries so you are less distracted. Thank God you are alive, even if you don't feel thankful at the moment. Only those in the cemetery have no problems. Thank God in advance for answers and responses to these problems, even though you don't see anything happening. Whether you choose to write in this book <u>or</u> an old notebook, now it's your turn…

What are my first loves? _____
_____
_____
_____
_____

How do these first loves control my life in healthy ways? …unhealthy ways?_____
_____
_____
_____
_____
_____
_____
_____

What wounds am I willing to offer God for tending and healing? _____
_____
_____
_____
_____
_____
_____
_____
_____
_____
_____
_____

## CONVERSATION WITH GOD
## #2

Dear GOD,

My goodness, time passes quickly! I am learning a lot! There are many dedicated people here who are not merely pew decorations. <u>Some</u> show a little weariness. <u>Some</u> get a little negative. <u>Some</u> are unable to do all they were once able to do. <u>Some</u> continue to amaze me with their ENERGY.

God let me ask <u>you</u>, **"Who would want to join this church?"** The neighborhood is <u>not</u> beautiful. We literally do ministry with "Bible in one hand, newspaper in the other." [*Theologian, Karl Barth*] However, the congregation is <u>not afraid</u> to get dirt under their fingernails. We are <u>not afraid</u> to get sticky. One cannot be part of the Children's Supper Hour without getting sticky!

This congregation is more than "keepers of the aquarium." [*George Hunter*] We know we are called to be fishers of men, women, boys and girls. We USE our building versus SAVING our building. I have always wondered, God, <u>what</u> were people saving the building for? Here, we use <u>and</u> revere the building. In answer to my earlier question, it seems to me… anyone who wants to make the world a better place… would <u>love</u> to be part of this church.

God, I can see you have given us a special mission. I know <u>you</u> <u>have</u> <u>far</u> <u>more</u> <u>invested</u> in this mission and in each person than we do. That brings more questions to mind: How do we <u>become</u> good stewards of your investment? How do we <u>both</u> protect <u>and</u> increase your investment?

### *Trust ME & just ask!*

**THAT SEEMS ALMOST <u>TOO</u> SIMPLE!** Yet, I have learned over the past 30 years—since I dedicated my life to you—<u>your</u> <u>ways</u> are relatively simple and unlike our complex ways.

You are right!  We need to continue to be good role models and mentors.  We need to ask for your guidance.  We need to lift up the prayer concerns of our parish, our city, our nation, and our world.  We need prayer warriors in order to do that!  Show me who they are!  Right again, we need to daily ask ourselves, **"How is it with my soul?"**

Keep me on track, God!  I am listening.

In Joy and In Peace,

*Sharon*

## ACTION REFLECTION:

This conversation asserts that God is saying, "Trust me!  Just ask me!"  Your written response to the questions is a way of asking.  Let go of all the complexities.  Simply share the things on your heart at this moment.  If these are not the questions for you, substitute with your own questions.  Trust God with all your cares, your confusion, and your feelings.  Trust God with your anger and your doubts.

What *has* God invested in me? _____
_____
_____
_____
_____
_____
_____
_____
_____
_____

What are my special gifts and abilities? _____

_____

_____

Who are my role models and mentors? _____

_____

_____

_____

Who has been looking to me as a role model? _____

_____

_____

How is it with my soul? _____

_____

_____

_____

_____

_____

Who might be a holy and good guide in soul matters? _____

_____

_____

_____

_____

_____

_____

_____

_____

Dear GOD,

Sometimes I am deeply burdened over the needs of the parish and the surrounding neighborhood. I know you are in charge, but sometimes it _feels_ as if the task is ALL mine. Thank you for correcting me! There is so much that needs to be done to make the neighborhood a safe place. Crime—violence, shootings, and drug dealing—has taken root. We believe we were called to stay and make a difference.

We are taking a STEP IN FAITH! You have invested a great deal in us. Our step in faith is to _invest in others_ and to PASS ON your blessings. We voted to invest in the church growth campaign! Some are wondering…"Our congregation is so small, what if we FAIL?" God, if we do nothing, we have already failed! What have we got to lose?

WE ARE COUNTING ON YOU to increase this investment. WE ARE COUNTING ON YOU to supply resources through Shalom Zone training to help solve problems that we do not know how to solve. BIG PROBLEMS! We will watch for _you_ working through it all.

As we seek your guidance: We SEE ourselves as an inspiration to other churches in the district and conference. We SEE ourselves as important in your scheme. We SEE ourselves as a NEW IMPROVED congregation. How do we get _from_ what we SEE… _to_ what we can BE?

### _One_ step at a time?
### _Are you sure there isn't a quicker way?_

I will be patient. In John 6:63, Jesus said, _"It is the spirit that gives life; the flesh is useless. The words that I have spoken to you are spirit and life."_ I guess what you are saying is… it will be _your_ _spirit_ that will give us life, _NOT_ our physical efforts. I trust your spirit. LEAD ON!

In Joy and In Peace,

*Sharon*


**ACTION REFLECTION:**

At the time this article was written, my world appeared to be falling apart. The same day someone broke into the church and stole food for the children's program was the same day my fiancé was arrested and thrown in jail. In a matter of minutes, all the meat for the supper hour was gone. In a matter of minutes, Daniel was cast into the unknown. In a matter of hours, we went from faithfully serving God to feeling totally abandoned and vulnerable.

I learned a lesson on vulnerability from a bunny that visits my back yard. Occasionally, the bunny would sit on my deck and munch carrot peels put out as a friendly gesture. The bunny was cautious of my movements just a few feet away on the other side of the sliding glass door. This cuddly looking creature lives with danger every day. This creature faced the unknown. Every day has the potential for good or danger. No creature is completely protected from danger or fear. Fear paralyzes. Fear has been defined as *False Evidence Appearing Real*. God seemed to be saying, "Have faith and take it <u>one</u> step at a time!" Now is your time to share with God as a trustworthy friend.

When have I felt as though my world was falling apart? _____

_____

_____

_____

_____

_____

_____

_____

What valuable insights did I learn from the experience? _____

_____

_____

_____

_____

_____

_____

How might I focus on God's Spirit and less on myself? _____

_____

_____

_____

_____

_____

_____

_____

_____

_____

_____

_____

_____

# CONVERSATION WITH GOD
## # 4

Dear GOD,

Y ou have been with me through many hard times.  I have seen your miracles.  You have been with the folks in this parish through many dark times.  They have shared some of the miracles you have done in their lives.  This sharing makes us stronger.

Before each miracle, there was some form of pain or struggle.  Life is never pain-free.  As in the Book of Job, people assume or imply, "What did you do to cause this?"  Or, like Job's wife, some urge us to turn away because "God has abandoned you."

God, when life is ROUGH and PAINFUL, it may feel as if you have abandoned us.  Nevertheless, faith is not the same as feelings.  While our feelings are very real, it is faith… you desire from us.

What I like about you, God, is that you can use all our stuff—our struggles, our weaknesses.  You even use opportunities we pass up.  You don't say, "I only want the GOOD STUFF, the good days."  YOU are a faithful GOD.  Why should we be any less?  YOU desire our praise.  Why should we offer anything less?

We are called to maintain our integrity through YOU.  When we keep our integrity, we experience freedom and peace through GRACE, through your Holy Spirit.  When your *"Son sets us free, we are free indeed."* [*John 8:36*]  We cannot be free until we learn to depend on you.  Here we are God.  No matter what happens in our personal life or our church life, we know we have hope in you.  Jesus knew that!  And like Jesus in his darkest hours, we only have to…

## *Wait three days!*

After three days, almost every situation looks different.

> Thank you for listening.
> Thank you for your presence, your peace.
> We are YOURS!!

Shalom,

**Sharon**

P.S. That would make a good sermon title: **WAIT THREE DAYS!**


## ACTION REFLECTION:

One need not look far to see tragedies. Tony's tragedy happened a few blocks from the church. He was an honor student at a local college. He was beaten and robbed of two dollars. Tony reported it to the police. As a result, the thieves beat him up again for reporting the incident. Two days later, Tony died. After the funeral, a dinner for Tony's family and friends was held in the fellowship hall of our church. His parents lost a beloved son. The neighborhood lost a fine young man.

When our world falls apart, we need hope. We want God to act NOW! Often, that doesn't happen. I found hope in my conversations with God. I connected with the pain outside the church walls. The neighborhood had fallen apart. No one seemed to know who or what to blame. My survival technique was to praise God in (not for) all things. This technique helps me rise above the situation and allow God to work.

Finding someone to share our struggle is a rare and wonderful thing. God wants *all our stuff*. God can use and transform all our stuff. Write down your stuff. In three days, look back at it. Leave it there! Don't pick it up!

What stuff do I need to dump on paper? _____

_____

_____

_____

What am I struggling with from the past? …the present? _____

_____

_____

_____

_____

For what situations do I need to "Wait three days"? _____

_____

_____

After three days, what is different in me? _____

_____

_____

_____

_____

_____

Dear GOD,

Your miracles were popping up <u>all</u> <u>over</u> last weekend at the FIRST SHALOM ZONE SUMMIT in Stamford, Connecticut! We gathered together—a rich mix of men and women, blacks, browns, and beiges (I am not white). There were people from Los Angeles, Philadelphia, Miami, Springfield, and many other cities. We came together seeking HOPE. There was more than enough to go around!

It was GOOD to hear of miracles in the '90s. It was GOOD to hear how <u>other</u> Shalom Zones in Los Angeles and Miami <u>are</u> making a difference! When the cesspools of our cities are being turned into gardens of hope—jobs, wholesome opportunities—YOU are <u>in</u> <u>there</u> working! We do not need any more young people to die or get hooked on drugs! Enough is enough! Help us believe. Help us learn to <u>see</u> our assets <u>both</u> inside <u>and</u> outside of the community. *"Create a clean heart in us, O God."* [*Psalm 51:10*] Cleanse us of negative ISMS—ageism, racism, classism, sexism, skepticism, criticism. We need clean hearts in order to believe…

## The sky's the limit when our heart is in it!

The Shalom training has given us tools with which to work. Remind us to PASS ON our blessings as we work to create SHALOM in Springfield. Help us to PASS ON the Shalom Zone Initiative to rural areas as well as urban areas. This can CATCH ON, CATCH FIRE, anywhere! Shalom is <u>not</u> <u>just</u> for the city! Any geographic area can focus on its assets and resources. Some feel it is risky to do this. I am re-minded of a story shared by Rev. Myron McCoy at the summit:

> An old farmer was sitting on his front porch, rocking in his rocking chair, puffing on his corn-cob pipe. A traveler stopped to rest and chat with the old farmer. He

asked, **"How's your cotton crop growin'?"** The farmer replied, "Ain't got none. I figured if I planted the cotton, the <u>boll</u> <u>weevil</u> would just take it. So, I didn't plant any cotton."

**"How's your corn crop growin'?"** "Ain't got none, I figured the <u>drought</u> would just take it. So, I didn't plant any corn."

The traveler persisted, **"Well, how's your potato crop growin'?"** "Ain't got none. I figured the <u>potato</u> <u>bug</u> would just infest the potatoes. So, I didn't plant any potatoes. I <u>just</u> played it SAFE!"

God, we can't afford to PLAY IT SAFE!

Shalom,

*Sharon*


## ACTION REFLECTION:

Don't let anyone steal your HOPE! Behind the scenes of this article, things seemed bleak. A promising young man's life was cut short. God was not whisking away our troubles! Regardless, I encourage you to <u>risk</u> hanging on to hope. Plant seeds of hope. Hope in God, not in the situation! Claim your hopes and your dreams. If you don't, don't expect someone else to do it for you. It's your turn…

What steals my hope? _____

_____

_____

_____

_____

_____

_____
_____
_____

What feeds my hope? _____
_____
_____
_____
_____

What "isms" do I need to admit I have? _____
_____
_____
_____
_____

What are my dreams? _____
_____
_____
_____
_____
_____
_____
_____
_____
_____

# CONVERSATION WITH GOD
## # 6

Dear GOD,

Our first evening **PEACE MARCH** is over. Over 100 persons walked the streets at night—singing songs, carrying flashlights—bringing light to the neighborhood. YOU walked with us. YOU spoke through us—to those who normally live behind locked doors after sunset—proclaiming PEACE for all. YOU declared the NEED for a safe place for children to grow up. YOU spoke out that it is <u>past time</u> for the crime and killing to stop.

It was GOOD. It was GOOD to have people join us—the mayor, politicians, sister churches, neighborhood people. It was GOOD to have **PEACE** on the front page of the newspaper and on the televised evening news. God, we have not abandoned our call to serve here in the inner city. We remain faithful. William H. Willimon tells the story:

> I was teaching my sixth grade class… telling them in <u>vivid</u> detail… of the arrest, trial, and crucifixion of Jesus. I was telling them how the soldiers carried him away, how Pilate and the people conspired to do Jesus in. A hand went up. "Yes, Bradford, what is it?"
>
> "I wanna know where was the rest of them?"
>
> "Rest of who, Bradford?"
>
> "Them disciples, where was they when things got rough for Jesus?"
>
> "The disciples? Oh, they were long gone." I replied.

"No, the rest of them," he persisted. "Where were they? What ever became of all them that he helped, the ones he healed? Now they had two good legs to walk, two good eyes to see. Where was they when them soldiers come to get Jesus?"

"Well, I don't know, Bradford."

"Yeah, you do," the little guy said softly. "They was just like most folks. They got what <u>they wanted</u>. Now they was gone."

*I AM HERE.*
*This is not the end.*
*It is only the beginning!*

Peace,

*Sharon*

## ACTION REFLECTION:

Walking with others at night through a neighborhood familiar with violence gave us hope. There are times when neighbors, family, or friends are unable to physically walk with us to give the support and hope we need. How do I find the support and hope I need? I go to my altar. My altar gives me hope. Just a few feet from the foot of my bed is a small stand with three shelves. After reading in <u>Simple Abundance</u> of Sarah Ban Breathnach's meditation about her altar, I made one of my own. I had considered doing this, but I didn't think I had a place for an altar. Sarah showed me I did. Be creative and you too, can have your own personal altar. My altar represents people who encourage me, love me, and believe in me. On my altar are: Votive candles, a # 1 Grandma necklace, a framed card I received when I graduated from college, biblical coins from the mother of a student in my first nursery class, a crystal crucifix, a kerosene lamp, a worry stone, a heart-shaped picture of my two daughters, an angel with a golden bird on her shoulder, five stones from Israel, our wedding picture and other precious memorabilia.

When I am deeply troubled, I don't pace or sit paralyzed any more. I shut the door. I light the lamp and candles; I sit on the floor and rest my back against the foot of the bed. I look at these things, which bring to mind treasured persons and events. The memories of these persons and events surround me with love. Love overcomes. Hope returns. I learned... ***one needs to give hope in order to have hope.*** As I sought inspiration for my readers, *I* was inspired. It is your turn...

Where can I build an altar of my own? _____

_____

What is my dark night experience? _____

_____

_____

What helped me get through it? _____

_____

_____

What difficult thing might God be asking me to do?_____

_____

_____

What can I do to give hope in order to have hope? _____

_____

_____

_____

_____

Dear GOD,

At the <u>end</u> of one year, the <u>beginning</u> of a New Year, I am certainly no Dr. Martin Luther King, Jr., but **I have dreams…**

**I have a dream…** of building trust in our neighborhood, of moving away from a welfare image to do ministry **"with"** instead of **"for"** persons.

**I have a dream…** of safe space, KIDSPACE—a place of laughter and joy, art and music, exercise and healthy snacks—instead of a basement where kids come twice a week to be served a free meal by adults on the other side of a counter.

**I have a dream…** of someday dissolving the hate, the violence, the prejudice, and people working together, living together as the song goes—"Ebony and ivory, live together on my piano keyboard, side-by-side in harmony."

**I have a dream…** of two rocking chairs in one corner of this KIDSPACE, with a beige grandparent and a black grandparent reading stories to children on their laps, side-by-side so that children will know we <u>can</u> live together in harmony.

**I have a dream…** of a PEOPLE EMPOWERMENT CENTER in our backyard (the former parsonage), and if we build it, as you say… "people will come." [*Field of Dreams*] People will come, one by one, receiving a hand-UP, not a handout. People will receive blessings, pass it on to others, and the goodness will spread!

**I have a dream…** of Shalom Zones spreading all over this city, this state, this nation, this world, and your kingdom will come… at last on earth.

*I HAVE A DREAM… that if I became one of you, people would be more understanding and more loving. My children would seek and follow my divine will. My kingdom would come on earth. Shalom would cover the earth and you would be whole. My children are slow to grasp my dream.*

GOD, don't give up on us. Help us turn these lofty dreams into reality. Help us build your kingdom. "If <u>YOU</u> build it, people will come."

**SHALOM,**

*Sharon*

**ACTION REFLECTION:**

   When it is dark, one needs to dream. Darkness may be one place where dreams are conceived. Sometimes reality is like a nightmare that doesn't go away! My niece, Tina, is a beautiful young woman. A few years ago, she was a passenger in the front seat of a car driven by a friend. There was a head-on collision. Tina had dreams of being an artist, of creating art to inspire others to have a closer connection with God. Tina's head shattered the windshield. She suffered broken facial bones, cuts. We were concerned she would lose her beauty. Instead, she experienced the loving care of her nurses and decided to become a nurse. Before she did so, I purchased two pieces of her work. One is a charcoal sketch of an open Bible, wire-rimmed glasses, and an old kerosene lamp. The other is a painting of Christ on the cross depicting the bleeding wounds with the words, "By his wounds, we are healed." Sometimes when I sit and look at those two pieces of Tina's artwork, it pulls me out of my self-pity. The fact that I love my niece makes a difference, I'm sure. I know the artist. Tina's dreams were diverted, but her artwork still inspires.

   We don't know what diversions we will encounter. Does it matter? What inspires you? Seek out pieces of art or photos that bring you solace. It's your turn to entertain a new dream...

What is my new dream? _____
_____
_____
_____
_____
_____

How do I see God in this dream? _____
_____
_____
_____
_____
_____

What would I need to ask of God in order to realize this dream?_____
_____
_____
_____
_____
_____
_____

Am I open to new dreams? _____
_____
_____
_____
_____
_____
_____

## CONVERSATION WITH GOD
## # 8

Dear GOD,

Does each month have a theme?  Last month seemed to be "LOVE" month.  This month seems to be "HOPE" month.  If miracles are a result of hoping in YOU, then every month should be HOPE month.  We are having miracles!

Volunteers cleaned the PEOPLE EMPOWERMENT CENTER.  One person was walking by and offered to help.  Five truckloads of old carpeting and junk were hauled away (free).  The wiring is almost complete.  We are ready to put in new windows and put on a new roof.  Lowering the ceilings will be the next task.  We keep praying YOU will show us the next step and you do.  God, we asked for a grant writer; three persons offered to help.  We went looking for grants; we found many possibilities.  We had no idea how to get this far; here we are.

God, we wondered how we would survive without $437 a month rent from the parsonage, and now we have a fundraiser ready to go.  We have EIGHT enthusiastic team leaders willing to lead us through a $10,000 finance campaign in five weeks.

God, I asked for one person to go with me to Birmingham, Alabama, for the conference on "Reclaiming Shalom in the Cities."  THREE will be going who are determined to come back armed with ideas and methods to transform our church and community.

God, we had a whole page of needs listed in the bulletin that volunteers have fulfilled.  People are praying for each other and for various projects.  People are still taking their prayer vitamins THREE TIMES A DAY:

***Breakfast — Give Thanks!***
***Lunch — Seek Guidance!***
***Supper — Offer Confession!***

As if that were not enough, beiges and blacks are marching, walking side-by-side in the Peace March and the Martin Luther King, Jr. March. And, sparks of HOPE are shining from the eyes of THREE more children at the Children's Supper Hour/KIDSPACE.

Miracles—I believe in miracles. I have seen them happen.

SHALOM & PRAISE TO YOU,

*Sharon*

**ACTION REFLECTION:**

In nature, beauty and growth are found in the most barren-looking places. In deserts, the cactus blooms. In the northwoods country, I have seen trees growing on the top of gigantic rocks. Beauty can spring out of the hardest situation. Look for beauty!

Where have I found beauty in hard, barren places? _____

_____

_____

_____

_____

_____

_____

_____

49

Where do I see a miracle just waiting to happen? _____

_____

_____

_____

_____

_____

_____

_____


What two or three people might be willing to help bring this miracle about? _____

_____

_____


How will I need God's help to bloom in my desert? _____

_____

_____

_____

_____

_____

_____

_____

_____

_____

_____

_____

# CONVERSATION WITH GOD
## # 9

Dear GOD,

I have heard people say, **"Oh, I used to go to that church."** I think to myself, "Too bad they are not here now, because… they are <u>missing out</u>!" Things are moving here… rolling like a WAVE, which is exactly how you move, isn't it, God! One WAVE rolled in last month!

God, I thank you for a person (whose name I do not know) who was part of this parish in the past. **This person <u>made</u> my day!** I do not even know <u>who</u> he or she is because Chaddock Children's Home must keep the confidentiality of the person who died in 1993 leaving a bequest to Chaddock for over $15,000 in honor of our church!

I <u>do</u> <u>know</u> this speaks well of our church. During difficult times, it is nice to know that someone, somewhere, out there—thought enough of us to make a bequest in our name.

God, it is <u>great</u> <u>to</u> <u>know</u> that even in our dying, we can rise to serve you, here on earth, in many ways. Each of us can do something to pass on and promote your work! WOW! I can do this, too! GOD…

Help us continue to make an impact for you.
Help us *ride the wave* of your Spirit moving through the SHALOM ZONE.
Help us continue to *thank you and praise you* all the way through,
around, and over the obstacles.

I have learned valuable lessons from the Shalom Zone and inner city ministry:
1. YOU ARE GREAT. Help us to praise you <u>even</u> <u>when</u> obstacles or tough times confront us. Praising you, the act of praising you, takes the focus off of ourselves and transports us over the obstacles.

2. Your Spirit moves in WAVES.  During the low times, we must <u>rest</u> in your Spirit.  We must <u>wait</u> until your Spirit crests and then <u>ride</u> <u>the</u> <u>wave</u>.  Things happen!  Doors open!  Obstacles are removed, and we <u>ride</u> <u>the</u> <u>wave</u>!  Thank you, God, for these valuable lessons!

**Shalom,**

*Sharon*


## ACTION REFLECTION:

At the Shalom training in Birmingham, I learned of God's *wave* rolling in and baptizing the city.  I had noticed that blessings seemed to come in bunches.  Then there would be a lull when nothing seemed to happen.  It was like beating one's head on a closed door.  I learned to stop beating my head on the closed door and wait for God's wave of blessing to roll in… and then ride the wave.  Your turn…

How have I experienced or watched for God's wave? _____
_____
_____
_____
_____
_____
_____

Waiting for the wave, what blessings will I praise God for that I've already received?_____
_____
_____
_____

_____

_____

_____

_____

_____

_____

I currently feel God's Holy Spirit in _____

_____

_____

_____

_____

_____

How might I practice "resting" until the wave of blessing rolls in?

_____

_____

_____

_____

_____

_____

_____

_____

_____

_____

_____

_____

_____

# CONVERSATION WITH GOD
## # 10

Dear GOD,

Your Special Sprouts are growing. SHALOM is growing. Shalom, the Hebrew word for peace, means <u>more</u> than the absence of conflict. It is everything that makes for our highest good. Shalom is a state of completeness in which people individually and collectively experience: Health, prosperity, security, oneness with neighbor, and spiritual renewal. SHALOM ZONES seek this wholeness.

God, when we pray, we do not know how you will answer. Some people do not believe you do answer. Last summer we prayed our Sunday school would grow. You gave us two beautiful children as seed. We tried almost everything. Finally, we gave up. You answered. We now have over 16 children in Sunday school! These "Special Sprouts" are so excited! After their first Youth & Children's Sunday, they turned in over <u>four</u> <u>pages</u> of notes on things they would like to learn and do in Sunday school and church! **THANK YOU!**

God, last summer the Children's Supper Hour/KIDSPACE was <u>not</u> a place of trust and mutual respect. It is now. Debbie, the former coordinator, noticed a dramatic change, "The kids used to come in and sit with their heads down and not speak." That has been replaced with humor, mutual respect and your **GOODNESS** <u>all</u> <u>over</u> the fellowship hall. I said, "Do you suppose the fact that we always start with prayer might have anything to do with it?" ***(I do! Thank you!)***

How I love these rainbow children! They are your Special Sprouts. They minister to me more than I minister to them. I love the following true story from D.C. Bensen's <u>Ministry</u> <u>of</u> <u>the</u> <u>Child</u>:

> While his parents listened to the sermon, a young boy busily colored a picture of Jesus and wrote in crooked letters across the page, "Jesus loves you." Despite his mother's embarrassment, the boy insisted on giving the picture to a man sitting farther along the pew.

A few weeks later, the man stopped the boy's mother and remarked that he was so thankful for that picture. He had been struggling with his wife's death and when he received the boy's picture, he felt God come into his heart.

Special Sprouts need TLC. Last week in Peoria, Bobby (age 11) was beaten and strangled. Friends called, "How do we get our SHALOM ZONE going? We need it!" God, for some we are too late. Forgive us. Have mercy on us. We will pray for Bobby's family and our sister SHALOM ZONE in Peoria.

Thank you for listening,

*Sharon*


## ACTION REFLECTION:

Seeds germinate in the darkness of the soil. Not all darkness is bad. When bad things happen we tend to ask, "Why?" The "why" habit distracts us from asking a positive question: What am I going to do differently as a result of this painful experience? Before our experience with injustice in the legal system, I was not concerned with injustice. I was not concerned with the incarcerated. I did not know how plea bargaining could be used and abused. Life looks very different from this angle. Your turn…

What is sprouting forth in my life? _____

_____

_____

_____

_____

_____

_____

Who are some of the special sprouts in my life? _____
_____
_____
_____

How will I nurture and care for them? _____
_____
_____
_____
_____

Who and what helps nurture me? _____
_____
_____
_____
_____

Where do I need to seek more support? _____
_____
_____

What am I going to do differently as a result of a painful experience? _____
_____
_____
_____
_____
_____
_____

Dear GOD,

As I sit in my backyard looking over my Garden of Shalom which I started last fall, I see evidence of those efforts. A friend helped me plant bulbs and dry "stringy-looking things" that I did not believe had any life in them. I planted them anyway. Some grew! Some did not. I am still watching. Maybe new life will emerge. I can HOPE. This is my *corner of peace*. This is my sunset-watching spot where I reflect on where YOU were in this day (my theology at sunset).

This week, quite unexpectedly, I was asked to talk with four confirmation students and their pastor from a rural church. They wanted to know about Shalom Zones. I met them in the parking lot and pointed out the Shalom Banner: **Peace to the Neighborhood.** I spoke of the joint efforts with our sister church. I spoke of our congregation being mostly Caucasian and the other church being mostly African American and how we enjoy working together. Love is growing here because of our relationship. I went on to say that several of the Peace Marches started right from this parking lot. They seemed very interested.

They noticed the alarm system signs. I said, "Yes, we have a security system. We lock our church doors because there are always a few persons willing to cross legal boundaries. However, the neighborhood feels much safer. PLUS, we know more of our neighbors than we did before."

We went inside. I showed them our sanctuary and the banner our Sunday school children had just completed. I told them, "Last summer, all summer, we had only two children. Now we have 30." The five guests looked at our food room (robbed prior to the security system), pictures of the Children's Supper Hour/KIDSPACE children, and kitchen. They noted, "It's just like our church." It was time to leave.

I asked, "Now do you understand what a 'Shalom Zone' is?" (They were thinking.)
One member of the group said:

## "A Shalom Zone is like *hugging* the neighborhood."

Thank you, God, for sending them! Thank you that Shalom is spreading. Shalom is growing, slowly, silently, steadily, as in my Garden of Shalom.

Shalom,

*Sharon*


**ACTION REFLECTION:**

The friend who helped plant my "Garden of Shalom" is now my husband. Together we planted vegetables and flowers. Months later the fresh food and beauty nurtured both body and soul. What had appeared to be dead seeds and bulbs, grew and produced *good* things. What seemed hopeless and painful during our trials blossomed into a beautiful testimony of love, hope, and deeper faith. Our garden is our sanctuary for reflecting on our blessings. It is a place to enjoy the sunsets. It is a place to be hugged by God and to heal. At the time article # 11 was written, we were both healing from Daniel's double attempt at suicide after our attorney badgered him to plea bargain. When you are out of money, you are advised to plea bargain.

We are called to share in Christ's suffering. Never again would we go through Holy Week without remembering this experience. Our experience with the legal system seemed far too similar to that of Jesus in the Garden of Gethsemane—betrayed, arrested, and abandoned. At the trial he was accused by false witnesses and then crucified. We have discovered it is an honor to share in his suffering.

What sufferings do I share with Christ?_____
_____
_____
_____

What areas of my life need a "security system"?_____
_____
_____
_____

What time and place do I feel closest to God? _____
_____
_____
_____

What can I do to stop worldly pessimism from stripping away my blessings? _____
_____
_____
_____

Where can I plant a garden of peace, healing, and hope? _____
_____
_____
_____
_____
_____
_____

# CONVERSATION WITH GOD
## # 12

Dear GOD,

I have declared this month: Seeing Jesus Month. I wish, as you do, that we all knew Jesus. We would not have to seek or spread SHALOM because SHALOM would already be here.

It is one of my favorite things to do—see Jesus! When I look back through my day, usually at sunset— *He was there!* As in the walk to Emmaus in Luke 24:31, "Then their eyes were opened, and they recognized him; and he vanished from their sight."

*He was there* in the compassion of an old friend, in the voice on the other end of the phone sharing a miracle, and in the peaceful smile of someone in the grip of cancer.

*Jesus was there* in the voice of a brave little boy about to undergo anesthesia for one of many surgeries: "Now I lay me down to sleep, I pray the Lord my soul to keep."

*Jesus was there* in the eyes of people who are genuinely sorry for hurting someone and in the eyes of those doing the forgiving. *Jesus was there!*

*Jesus was there* in the young people taking part in the "Sarah and Abraham" song, and in the hands of the one holding the drumsticks giving us a new beat to worship YOU. Jesus was there in the eyes of a proud loving mother, father, and grandparent.

The more we SEE Jesus, the more our church will turn from a FORTRESS into an OASIS. The more we SEE Jesus, the more the walls of fear will come down and we will become the life-giving, nurturing body of Christ we need to be.

Jesus does not dwell merely within the walls of a church building. Jesus walks the streets of South Grand and Capitol Avenue, Brown and Kansas Street. Sometimes, we do not see him, but he is there. And, he *loves* the people of this city as well as the people in the suburbs and the small towns.

For those who have not yet found Jesus, I pray YOU will help them find Him. Pull them closer to you. I know you care. *I KNOW...THAT I KNOW... THAT I KNOW!*

SHALOM!

*Sharon*


## ACTION REFLECTION:

Don't I sound full of hope? Let me tell you what preceded this: A two and a half-day trial with a guilty verdict! Hearing that verdict ripped me with pain comparable to what I felt when I heard my little boy (age two) had been killed in an auto accident. You never forget that pain! Life is not always fair. Injustice is alive; I studied injustice personally and in my parish. We were in a wilderness.

Life seemed absolutely barren. Even Jesus was led into the wilderness [*Matthew 4:1-11 and Mark 1:12-13*]. Don't be deceived into believing God does not care when we are going through a wilderness. Remember, the angels came and ministered to Jesus! The angels ministered to us! We were able to recognize angels ministering to us, *angels standing with us*. We were not alone.

What instances of "knowing" have I had? _____

_____

_____

_____

_____

Where have I seen Jesus this week? _____

_____

_____

_____

_____

_____

_____

_____

Where might I expect to see Jesus? _____

_____

_____

_____

_____

_____

_____

How might you be the "Jesus" other people need to see? _____

_____

_____

_____

_____

_____

_____

_____

_____

_____

_____

# CONVERSATION WITH GOD
## # 13

Dear GOD,

When it is HOT, a cool glass of ice water is SO refreshing! This water reminds me of the story of Jesus with the "Woman at the Well" in John 4:1-42. Through a brief encounter with Jesus, the Samaritan woman launched a town revival.

God, it is amazing that an old well (Jacob's well) in the presence of Jesus, helped launch a revival. The location seems so unlikely. It seems unlikely you would empower those who have tarnished lives to impact others. *(Oh, yes, I would! I do!)*

God, could it be… that an old, tired church… could become an OASIS from which new life and transformation could spring forth? To many persons, this seems so unlikely.

Could it be… that many persons in our neighborhood with tarnished lives will be able to impact others as in the story of the "Woman at the Well?"

God, could it be… that as Jesus became weary, sat down beside Jacob's well, those who came near him… were refreshed and made brand new? Some would say, "I don't believe it! It is just a well. He is just a man."

God, in the story all that one had to do was sit with Jesus, rest with Jesus, and ask for the "living water." This seems just TOO EASY. Yet, I KNOW this is true, for I have been to the well with Jesus. He is no ordinary man! There are springs of "living water" welling up inside me and inside many others here. The "living water" is here!

## I AM the oasis!  Send your parched people to the oasis!

Pour out your living water upon the parched city streets—the lost, the addicted, the hopeless.  Pour out your living water upon your servants!  People need Jesus to quench their thirst!  Refresh and renew us!  Heal us and make us whole!

Shalom,

*Sharon*


## ACTION REFLECTION:

I hope you see… regardless of what is happening in your life… God cares!  I was parched; God wasn't.  We learned… sometimes you just lose your case!  Six percent of the incarcerated are in prison because they lost their case!  Sometimes our worst nightmare becomes reality!  Focusing on God, rather than on the nightmare, helped me survive.  Focusing on God brings the darkness and fear into the light, into a holy place.  My greatest battle is getting the focus <u>off</u> of my self, my self-pity.  God is merciful and helps me do this when I ask.  Now, it's your turn…

Where would I prefer to dwell, on the negative <u>or</u> the positive? _____

_____

_____

_____

_____

_____

_____

_____

Where do I find refreshment in the dog days of summer? _____

_____

_____

_____

How do I refresh my parched soul? _____

_____

_____

_____

_____

_____

How does the living water taste? _____

_____

_____

What do I do when I do everything right and I still lose? _____

_____

_____

_____

_____

_____

_____

_____

_____

_____

Dear GOD,

I n looking back over this year, appointed to serve and celebrate inner city ministry, it has been one of the **best years** of my life. It has been one of the **most difficult years** of my life! A deeply fulfilled life seems to walk through the valleys <u>and</u> over the mountains. Sometimes having an ATTITUDE OF GRATITUDE escapes me. Sometimes I must simply ask, "How does one do that?" And YOU remind me…

### *Enter into MY presence with praise and thanksgiving.*
### *Give thanks and praise for who I AM.* [*Psalm 100:4, Sharon's version*]

When I don't want to give you praise and thanksgiving for what I'm going through, YOU remind me …

### *Do it anyway.*

**I have learned** over the years, your peace is just around the corner. Turn the corner!
**I have learned** an ATTITUDE OF GRATITUDE turns lemons into lemonade. Life may throw evil at us, but your GRACE, your Holy Spirit is able to resurrect the ashes of our lives.
**I have learned** you never promised life would be fair or just. You only promised never to leave us.
**I have learned** when I give thanks in the face of problems… you show me possibilities.

God, I am grateful to be here in the city, grateful to serve this Community of Shalom, grateful to *"Seek the Shalom of the city."* [*Jeremiah 29:7*] God, I am grateful, even though our ministry is not easy. This ministry has depth. I am grateful for your presence. I am never alone. No one need ever be alone.

God, show us those who feel cut off from you. Help us extend your love, peace, and joy. Only with your help do we build SHALOM.

THANKS,

*Sharon*


## ACTION REFLECTION:

I wrote this column while drawing from the wells of faith in God. Daniel was incarcerated. I was in shock trying to deal with the reality: THIS COULD HAPPEN TO INNOCENT PERSONS! During this time, a heat wave killed over 600 people. I'm glad I <u>didn't</u> <u>know</u> Daniel was in a two-man cell with no air conditioning and no moving air. He was allowed only two showers in ten days. He wore a dirty yellow jumpsuit another man had just taken off. Sweat soaked his two-inch thick mattress and never did dry out. Daniel's "cellie" was his angel. This kind cellmate gave him advice on how to stay alive and out of trouble. This cellmate was a "GD" (Gangster Disciple), but he had a good heart.

When it is difficult to praise God, look for things of beauty, moments of beauty. Beauty helps me get unstuck. Take time to write, to express honestly to God, the answers to these questions:

What beauty do I see around me? _____

_____

_____

_____

_____

_____

_____

_____

What moments of beauty do I remember? _____

_____

_____

_____

_____

_____

_____

_____

What chokes off my gratitude? _____

_____

_____

_____

_____

_____

_____

What can I do to avoid this from happening?

_____

_____

_____

_____

_____

_____

_____

_____

_____

_____

# CONVERSATION WITH GOD
## # 15

Dear GOD,

B e patient with me; YOU seem <u>too</u> BIG.  I need someone smaller; I need someone who I know has *been there*!  **Jesus KNOWS** life has traps, hardships, disease, lies.  He **KNOWS** "the blackest of all lies is a half-truth, for it is the most difficult to disprove." [*NPR, origin unknown*]

> **Jesus KNOWS** "bad things happen to good people." [*H. Kushner*]
> **Jesus KNOWS** the daily turmoil and the search for peace.
> **Jesus KNOWS** the <u>feeling</u> of being forsaken.
> **Jesus KNOWS** we must turn from asking, "<u>WHY</u> <u>ME</u>?" to asking:

> > How can <u>I</u> make a difference?
> > What have I <u>learned</u> that I am able to <u>pass</u> <u>on</u>?
> > How do I <u>show</u> that I care?

Asking these questions changes the <u>focus</u> from myself to the kingdom of God.  Focus on God in the eye of the storm.  I am reminded, God, of your angels (both in heavenly and human form) who have stood with me over the years, and this past year…

- Only days before my best friend attempted suicide, an angel was seen <u>standing</u> <u>behind</u> me in the pulpit during worship.
- An angel in human form <u>sat</u> <u>right</u> <u>up</u> <u>front</u> in worship.  He came all the way from New Orleans to tell me: "I have a message for you from the Book of James."
  > ***Consider it pure joy, my sisters and brothers, whenever you face trials of many kinds, because you know the testing of your faith develops perseverance.*** [*James 1:2, 3*]

God, I take my <u>stand</u> <u>with</u> <u>angels</u> and the "great cloud of witnesses" [*Hebrews 12:1*] who constantly surround me on a different level of life as I know it.

**I have learned…**
- I <u>do</u> <u>not</u> let anyone strip me of my integrity or honor.
- I am <u>set</u> <u>free</u> by being true to YOU and true to myself.
- I can HEAR another's pain and refrain from advice.

**I can help…**
- By <u>not</u> assuming I understand someone else's situation.
- By praying, not saying I will pray, but praying… by phone, by mail (write a prayer), in person NOW, not later.
- By saying, "I care…(meaning) I stand <u>with</u> you!"

In Joy and In Peace…

*Sharon*


**ACTION REFLECTION:**

I cut a small piece of yellow ribbon, folded it, stuck an angel pin through the center, and wore it daily. I was taking my stand with angels in worshiping God *no matter what*. I was taking my stand with angels, taking a stand <u>for</u> justice wherever injustice was found. I didn't do it alone. I learned to appreciate the nuggets of wisdom collected in the wilderness. Your turn…

What do I appreciate? _____

_____

_____

What do I KNOW about myself? _____

_____

_____

_____

_____

_____

What do I KNOW about Jesus? _____

_____

_____

_____

What do I KNOW about God? _____

_____

_____

_____

What do I KNOW about God's Holy Spirit? _____

_____

_____

_____

_____

# CONVERSATION WITH GOD
## # 16

Dear GOD,

Fall is my **FAVORITE** time of year! I love the cool weather with a "kiss of summer" still in each day. Fall is an expression of your **JOY,** with colors exploding all over the place. It is a beautiful time of the year!

With colorful bursts of **JOY**, it is easier to forget our trials, our problems. James (the oldest of Jesus' brothers) wrote the Book of James and had a different outlook on trials. God, I was truly blessed by the man who came all the way from New Orleans with a message for me from James!

> ***Consider it pure joy, my sisters and brothers, whenever you face trials of many kinds, because you know the testing of your faith develops perseverance.*** [*James 1:2,3*]

We would not have our depth of JOY without the trials, which bring out our truer, deeper colors. Without trials, our roots would not grow deeper in order to stabilize our being.

**IN FALL COLORS:** I see your **JOY**, I see our roots, I celebrate the trials as our Purple Hearts, our badges of honor. We are w-o-n for Christ, because we are one with Christ. Until we have been tested, we do not know of what we are made. That goes for individuals, as well as churches.

The annual planning event has made me aware… from where we have come… to where we are. There are many in this congregation—inside and outside the church walls—who have won their Purple Heart, their badge of courage, by believing in Jesus Christ, by taking their stand with Christ, no matter what. The past few years there have been many trials. Trials turn into possibilities because we hold fast to our roots in Christ.

The planning event reminds me of our <u>vibrant</u> <u>worship</u> each Sunday. It reminds me this tiny congregation has an <u>extraordinary</u> <u>outreach</u> through the Children's Supper Hour/KIDSPACE, the People Empowerment Center, Inc., the SHALOM ZONE with our sister church, and the fundraisers (especially the Barbeque and Summer Festival).

Wear those Purple Hearts (your cross, your life experiences) <u>knowing</u>... Jesus does **resurrections**, <u>not</u> funerals!

In Joy and Shalom!

*Sharon*


## ACTION REFLECTION:

While others may try to trash our lives and throw mud on us, I believe in resurrections. I believe whoever said undeserved suffering is redemptive is only partly correct. I am concerned for those who do not know how to seek redemption from their suffering. I believe teaching people to connect with the Holy Spirit is part of the process. I believe we are more courageous than we think we are. I believe God is the worker of marvels. Regardless of feeling like a "crash and burn" survivor, my ordination class elected me to be carrier of the "Torch of Faith" for our class. Some of the mud just washed off. Now it's your turn. Let's start with the positive...

What is my favorite time of year? Why?_____

_____

_____

_____

_____

_____

What "joy" times do I have? _____

_____
_____
_____
_____
_____
_____
_____

What trials can I allow God to turn into possibilities? _____

_____
_____
_____
_____
_____
_____
_____
_____

Have I earned my "Purple Heart"?  If so, these are my Purple Heart experiences: _____

_____
_____
_____
_____
_____
_____
_____
_____

# CONVERSATION WITH GOD
## # 17

Dear GOD,

I do not know what I would do or be if I could not be present with you in journaling, in praise, in pleading, in confession, in joy, in tears, in love, in peace. **YOU** are my source, my refuge, my friend, my today, my tomorrow. Help me hang on to a healthy attitude in loving and serving you. Help me remember…

## *Attitudes are contagious!*
## *Is my attitude worth catching?*

**YOU KNOW** how we complain about our world today. Everyone has an opinion!
**YOU KNOW** that unless we are willing to be part of the solution, we are part of the problem.
**I KNOW** you do not have much patience with complainers (Check out Exodus 15, 17, Numbers 11:1).

Remind us, God, that Jesus is **YOUR OPINION**. Remind us, God, to thank YOU for Jesus Christ, and **YOUR OPINION**. Remind us to ask:

## *What did Jesus say and do?*
## *And, why did he say and do it?*

It is time for everyone (clergy, churched, unchurched) to stop our whining and count our blessings. In other words, stop focusing on what we don't have, and start focusing on what **WE DO HAVE**.

God, I am grateful that I have never had to be confined to a wheelchair. Remind <u>everyone</u> (reading this right now) that we would not sit in a wheelchair long… before we would be pleading to be out of it. We would promise you anything! **HOW QUICKLY WE FORGET OUR PROMISES!**

Keep my attitude healthy! I love serving you. Help me focus on the GOOD without <u>dwelling</u> on the bad, which can be worshipping evil. Help us discover what it is you have given us to do. I firmly believe if people clearly knew what to do, they would do it!

Yes, God, our attitudes and excuses are HOGWASH! You know it! You gave each of us something to do for you. What is more, **YOU EXPECT** us to be doing it! You are **LIFE**, daily life and eternal life. I thank you for this day, for this moment to serve you.

In Joy and Shalom,

*Sharon*


**ACTION REFLECTION:**

   We can give our bad attitudes to God for transformation. Isn't that amazing? Honestly consider the following sentences and write your conversation with God.

   People who know me would say I have a _____ attitude.
   I have this attitude because of _____.
   God has promised me _____.
   I expect _____ from God.

76

# CONVERSATION WITH GOD
## # 18

Dear GOD,

O ur spirits <u>are</u> rising!  You are **GOOD**!  Together we are facing the deeper questions of life, such as:
How <u>do</u> I grow old gracefully? …face death? …face life around me?
What do I do about depression and negativity poisoning the Body of Christ?
How <u>do</u> I find hope, find the positive, find **CHRIST** <u>in</u> <u>all</u> <u>I</u> <u>do</u>?

I know, **LORD**, that some people need antidepressants, counseling, inner and physical healing.  Some need spiritual healing, inner security, soul healing.  I know we need you!

God, we can't walk this road alone.  Each life, as was the birth and life of Jesus, is a **GIFT**, a life to be shared.  We receive life's greatest moments <u>when</u> <u>we</u> <u>give</u> the Jesus in us… away.  First, we receive it from **CHRIST**, then we share his kindness, compassion, his reliability.  Others let us down; <u>he</u> is the <u>best</u> of all friends.

God, many persons practice negativity, separation, dis-unity without realizing it:
Goodwill is unity:   Ill will is separation.
Love is unity:   Hate is separation.
Hope is unity:   Fear is separation. [*Kimbro, Oct. 5*]

God, thank you for that insight and this modern day parable from Kimbro:

One day a little girl from an African tribe wandered off into the tall jungle grass.  She couldn't be found, though the tribe searched several days.  Then a little boy got an idea.  He suggested… <u>everyone</u> <u>hold</u> <u>hands</u> and walk through the grass together.  Surprisingly, the girl was found, but due to her exposure to the damp evening air… she died.  In his anguish and through tears, her little playmate cried, **"If only we had held hands sooner."**

God, we can hold hands NOW.  We can face these questions.  With Christ, we can walk hand in hand—large church, small church; east side, west side; beige hand, deep bronze hand; male, female; adult, child.  God, you have not asked us to do that which we cannot do.  Spirits <u>are</u> rising!

### *We are holding hands now.*

In Joy, In Peace… Shalom,

*Sharon*

**ACTION REFLECTION:**

  Imagine this scene after I shared the above parable in a sermon…  From that day on, after the benediction, hands reached out to the person standing closest… all across the sanctuary.  Adults and children made a living chain of hope.  This chain zigzagged across the center aisle and connected all those present.  Arms were outstretched and hands clasped.  Daniel and I held hands in the visiting room in the prison.  I spent Thanksgiving, Christmas, and all major holidays at the prison.  The visiting room was quite different from my previous white middle-class holiday celebrations.  We learned new insights.  These are your questions to consider…

  Who needs my "hand" on life's path? _____
_____
_____
_____
_____

Where is God... in life and death issues? _____

_____

_____

_____

_____

_____

Where is God... in the aging process? _____

_____

_____

_____

_____

_____

What is the best part of getting older? _____

_____

_____

_____

_____

_____

What is the most troublesome part of getting older? _____

_____

_____

_____

_____

_____

_____

Dear God,

There is a great difference between yesterday and today, between last year and this year. We can look at yesterday and realize we cannot change yesterday. We can <u>learn</u> from all we did, failed to do, or did not get done, but we cannot win in the game of "catch-up." We must let go of yesterday and move on to LIVE fully <u>today</u>. We can learn from last year and years before, but we cannot change those years. We must let go and LIVE fully <u>NOW</u>.

In our letting go, let us for a sacred moment savor the joys of the past. Let us savor the wonderful individuals YOU have sent to touch our lives. A warm glow spreads through our souls as we do this. (Feel it?) Your light, your EPIPHANY, fills our souls. Without you, we would not have a soul. We would not have life, light, joy, dreams, hope, or love. How does one say thank you for life?

God, the only way I know to thank you, is to PASS ON the gifts YOU have given us. First, together we <u>appreciate</u>, we <u>celebrate</u>, we <u>collaborate.</u> Then, we <u>generate</u> new life in Christ. I am reminded as I sing "This Is a Day of New Beginnings" by Brian Wren:

This is a day of new beginnings,
Time to remember and move on,
Time to believe what love is bringing,
Laying to rest the pain that's gone (stanza 1).

Christ is alive, and goes before us
To show and share what love can do.
This is a day of new beginnings;
Our God is making all things new (stanza 4).

God, this hymn has had a healing effect on my life. It has touched my pain; it has helped heal my brokenness. It reinforces my belief that you always have **something far better** for us than what we think we need.

God, my prayer for those reading this is… the words will be healing. I pray they will allow Christ to touch their pain, to heal their brokenness, to give them **something far better** than what they think they need. Then, let's PASS IT ON to others <u>every</u> day.

IN JOY and IN PEACE… SHALOM,

*Sharon*


## ACTION REFLECTION:

When our journey takes an unanticipated curve, it isn't always easy to be enthusiastic about it. Sometimes these unexpected curves steal my joy. How about you?

What is keeping me from enjoying this moment, this day? _____
_____
_____
_____
_____
_____

As I live my life, I will _____
_____
_____

I would like to begin _____

I would like to see an end to _____

How do I say "Thank You" for life? _____

Dear God,

Whoever said, **"Little things mean a lot!"** was absolutely correct.  Little things have meant a lot to me:  Bouquets of dandelions, homemade Valentines, the scribbled "I love you, Mom," phone calls and notes of encouragement, spontaneous love poems, gentle hugs.

How I love to hear people say these few words to others:  "I am so proud of you!"  "Good job!"  "We appreciate you!"  "What would we do without you?"  "I admire how you do that."  "Thank you!"  Little things do make a difference!

God, in regard to the tragic accident in which Angela's life was snuffed out and Clarissa was seriously hurt, I overheard comments:  "How tragic, how sad!"  "Is that 'our' Clarissa?"  "Isn't that 'our girl', the one who sings?"  Such comments show caring and inclusion.  YES, she's "our girl" and we love her and are praying for her complete recovery so she can sing again and again.  And, Omar is "our Omar," the one who survived a serious gunshot wound and who is now helping lead the Boy Scouts.  **Little things mean a lot...** especially in times of need!

**Little things can hurt.**  For instance, comments we say to others we would not want said to us:  "You only need 2 cookies!"  "Don't give any to the black kids."  "Look at all those white kids."  Age-old annoyances, petty jealousies, keep the wounds open.  It seems, God, we humans would rather pick at wounds than love each other as you intended.

**Little things can heal**, as spoonfuls of medicine help heal:  Asking, "What's your name?"  Saying, "I'm sorry."  "I believe there is GOOD in you."  "I SEE good in you!"  "Jesus loves you."  Asking, "What would Jesus do?"

God, remind us to spoon-feed wise words, kind deeds, notes of encouragement. Let us begin, God, with YOU. <u>You</u> appreciate little things we do for you and the times we say:

I don't know what I would do without you!　　***(You smile)***
Thank you for loving me, warts and all.　　　***(You smile)***
Thank you for turning my life around!　　　　***(You smile)***

You NEVER get tired of hearing us say these things to you or hearing us say them to our brothers and sisters in your family. I LOVE YOU!

Sharon


## ACTION REFLECTION:

Take time to ponder and write your honest thoughts to God. Share your guilty feelings, your wounds, your joys. Ponder the small victories and rewards in life.

What little things have meant a lot to me? _____

_____

_____

_____

_____

_____

_____

_____

_____

_____

_____

The praise of others makes me feel _____

_____

_____

_____

_____

_____

This is because _____

_____

_____

_____

_____

_____

Someone worthy of my praise is _____

_____

_____

_____

_____

_____

Who needs my praise? _____

_____

_____

_____

_____

_____

_____

# CONVERSATION WITH GOD
## # 21

Dear God,

I am always grateful for spring! When we are surrounded with flu, coughs, colds, snow, and freezing wind, winter can be discouraging! There is a legend…

> A man found the barn where Satan kept his seeds ready to be sown in the human heart, and on finding the *seeds of discouragement* more numerous than others, he learned those seeds could be made to grow almost anywhere. When Satan was questioned, he reluctantly admitted there is <u>one</u> place he could never get them to thrive.
>
> "And where is that?" asked the man.
> Satan replied, "In the heart of a grateful man." [*Kimbro*]

### *Be grateful for what you have,*
### *Not regretful for what you haven't.*

**I am practicing.** I am grateful for our journey with Christ through the Bible Study on the Gospel of Mark. I am grateful for questions we need to ask:

What disturbs me about this text?
With which character do I identify? Why?
How does this text apply to me?

I am grateful for tough, meaningful questions (still practicing). I am grateful for a time of penance to: Confess, repent, forgive and receive forgiveness in Christ's name. More questions…

What do I (you) need to confess?
What do we, the Body of Christ, need to confess?

    Okay, here goes_____(invisible ink).

Seriously, God, you know our hearts and souls need times of penance, to literally SPRING CLEAN our SOULS. I am grateful for these times.

I am grateful for the faith you have given me in small increments. You rarely allow your disciples to see and have more faith than it takes to go a few more steps. That is the best way to cultivate our faith and grow deep roots, isn't it.

### *YES!*

God, help me be a planter of seeds of faith!
God, help me plant SHALOM!

*Sharon*


## ACTION REFLECTION:

    Everyone gets discouraged. We can fixate on discouragement and remain stuck. Face the fact that this does happen. Name it and move on. Believe in resurrections!

    These persons and things discourage me_____
_____
_____
_____
_____

God, please help me overcome discouragement in the area of _____

_____

_____

_____

_____

_____

_____

_____

In order to overcome such discouragement, I am willing to _____

_____

_____

_____

_____

_____

_____

_____

What am I grateful for, even in the midst of this discouragement? _____

_____

_____

_____

_____

_____

_____

_____

_____

_____

Dear God,

There is a saying, "If you can't beat them, join them." I hear:

WE MUST PROTECT THE INSTITUTION or there won't be…
WE MUST PRESERVE THESE CHURCH WALLS or there won't be…
WE MUST SAVE OURSELVES or we won't be here to…

Why, what would the world do without ALL <u>WE</u> have built up? (caution) What about it, God? What do you say?

*I did (do) join you!*
*Remember?!?*

Forgive me; forgive us. Help us empty ourselves—of OURSELVES—on our journey to the cross. Help us move beyond, to your RESURRECTION, and blessings.

*I can't bless the ungrateful.*
*To do so… would be to multiply ingratitude.*
(Oh…)

Then, God, show us <u>how</u> to become grateful and have glad hearts in the midst of our struggles and pain.

*Start with <u>one</u> holy moment you treasure.*
*Hold it! Hang on to it!*

Yeah, I see, I feel a HOLY glow melting "ingratitude" and "mean-spiritedness," both of which block blessings. I am holding onto this treasured moment.

IS MY TASK to help others find a flicker of gratitude, holiness, in their hearts and go from there? *(Yes)* Then, HOLY ONE, I ask you to multiply this tiny gift we give to you. It is our starting point, a jump-start, a renewal point, a turning point, a "stand up and walk" in JOY, a "get up off your sick bed" moment of HOPE!

God, help us move beyond…"all seems bleak and black." GOOD FRIDAY was a black page with a tiny dot of white (the goodness of your Son) written on a page of history. From Easter, you transform us to a tiny dot on a white page surrounded by your light.

As we humble ourselves and seek a HOLY MOMENT which you will bless and multiply, we see JESUS on Good Friday as one who was willing to join us in our darkness in order to ignite a HOLY spark of light, gladness, and hope. THANK YOU. Do not let anyone destroy our hope and joy. Humbly, I spread your JOY and...

SHALOM,

*Sharon*


**ACTION REFLECTION:**

One of my Holy Moments occurred in my living room. It was August, the anniversary of my son's death. I was depressed. It had been 25 years since Mike's death. Every year in August I would get depressed. As I leaned over to switch on a lamp, I heard an inner message: ***"You never had any part in the funeral plans."*** That was correct. I had gone directly to the hospital to be with Lori, who was four, and who was seriously injured in the same accident. Others did all of the planning of my son's funeral. God was giving me a cue to do something about it. As a pastor, I helped people plan funerals for their loved ones. I gathered my hymnals, paper, pen. I lit a candle and sat on the floor. I wrote to Michael of <u>all</u> the things I didn't get to do, all the things I would have done. I picked hymns that were meaningful to me. I wrote my "good-byes" to my two-year-old son. I held him in my arms one more time. I wept. This time the tears were healing. The presence of peace in my living room was so thick, as the expression goes, "You could cut it with a knife!" No more do I become depressed in August.

Take out a blank sheet of white paper. With a pen, make a small dot in the center. Pretend the dot represents you and your problems surrounded by light on the page. There is a lot more light than darkness, isn't there? Now, cut the dot out, leaving an inch-sized hole in the paper. Hold it up; look through the hole. We only see part of the situation. God sees the whole situation. No two persons are in exactly the same place spiritually, emotionally, intellectually, or physically. Ask God which questions or statements you need to respond to:

What causes me to get depressed? _____

_____

_____

_____

_____

_____

What do I need to do to overcome depression? _____

_____

_____

_____

_____

_____

_____

What do I need to do to change ungrateful habits? _____
_____
_____
_____
_____
_____
_____
_____

When have I helped multiply ingratitude?_____
_____
_____
_____

The thing I would most willingly work to preserve is _____
_____
_____
_____
_____

God, help me move beyond _____
_____
_____
_____

Some people I can join forces with in this matter are _____
_____
_____
_____

Dear GOD,

TODAY… I am a new person, not as I was yesterday, not as I will be tomorrow. TODAY… I begin anew with you, with Jesus Christ. New beginnings change us!

I AM CHANGED through meeting Lu Ann this week. I was showing her photos of the Children's Supper Hour/KIDSPACE and the fellowship hall where we eat, interact, create safe space with children. Lu Ann said, "This is great! I did not know this was here! How are you funded?" I responded, "It is like the 'loaves and fishes'; it is a miracle we do what we do on what we have to spend."

I AM CHANGED as I look directly into the eyes of Dion, a <u>challenging</u> boy at the Supper Hour, and say, "I see *GOOD* in you! God planted *GOOD* in you! Do not let anyone take it from you!" For a brief moment, I see in Dion's eyes that <u>knowing</u> of the GOOD in himself. I AM CHANGED.

I AM CHANGED because an insurance agent from the parish shared this story about Larry, who lives in the decaying city housing development:

Larry was dirty, hair a mess, on drugs. The agent told Larry, "I am going to <u>pray</u> for you for <u>six</u> months, <u>three</u> times a day. <u>God</u> <u>loves</u> <u>you</u>."

Months went by. The agent stopped to see Larry's Mom about insurance and a young man was in the living room who sort of… looked like Larry. The young man was smiling, clean, handsome. The agent said, "Are you Larry's brother? You look a little like Larry."

The young man said, "I <u>am</u> Larry. I found Christ at a revival. I <u>am</u> Larry."

God, I am learning to see YOU, to see **GOOD** in people. I am learning that <u>no one</u> race or gender has the franchise on truth. <u>No one</u> has the franchise on suffering, ignorance, hate, and violence. <u>No one</u> has the copyright on PEACE or SHALOM.

Remind us, God, that YOU supply our needs. Remind us not to let anyone take the GOOD from us. Remind us to pull together in love and walk <u>with</u> our rainbow sisters and brothers. Remind us daily to be born anew!

IN PEACE and IN JOY,

*Sharon*


## ACTION REFLECTION:

Today is your new beginning. We resist change. However, we do not like boredom. Life <u>is</u> change. These questions are for you…

What has God changed in me? _____

_____

_____

_____


Who have I seen God change? _____

_____

_____

_____

_____

How do I see GOOD in myself? _____

_____
_____
_____
_____
_____

How do I see GOOD in others? _____

_____
_____
_____
_____
_____

How is this goodness genuine and consistent? _____

_____
_____
_____
_____
_____
_____
_____

Dear GOD,

I am embarrassed. My lack of faith has given allegiance to "worry." Precious hours have been wasted on THIS or THAT. I could have been, should have been praying and wondering:

Have I done all I need to do in each situation?

How will YOU work in this situation?

What are YOU doing secretly?

I could have been, should have been thanking you for what YOU have done and will do. When YOU build, YOU build <u>rock solid</u>! How many times must I learn this lesson? ENOUGH IS ENOUGH! YOU ARE ENOUGH! YOU are all I need.

LORD, at a meeting a woman stood up and read from Ecclesiastes 3.

There is a time for everything, and a season for every activity under heaven:

A time to be born and a time to die…

A time to tear down and a time to build…

A time for THIS and a time for THAT…. [*my version*]

## *And it doesn't say, "A time to worry!"*

I HEARD YOU. No one else speaks so quietly with such power. I give things, situations, POWER over me by dwelling on them. Your voice is tearing down "worry walls" that I have built. Rebuild this house with walls of faith. In my new dwelling there is an appreciation room for all seasons, seasons of rest, and seasons of growth. There is a gratitude room. In that room, I take a pen and notebook every night before I go to bed and write down <u>five</u> things for which I am grateful that day. I am grateful for:

1   The first Shalom honorees:  Annie and Albert.
2   The "Shalom Feed Yourself" program:  **70** gardens in the Shalom Zone!
3   The Appreciation Dinner for 42 volunteers who transformed the old parsonage into the People Empowerment Center!
4   Two new babies to baptize!
5   The growing enthusiasm in the Shalom Zone!

LORD, time spent in gratitude is far more rewarding and filling for my soul than time spent on the "**w**" word.  *Right!*

Shalom,

*Sharon*


## ACTION REFLECTION:

A good friend said to me… "David only needed ONE of the five stones he picked up to kill Goliath." God provides stones to deal with our Goliaths.  We don't need heavy artillery.  People need God!  It is good to be honest.  Even *with* God, we worry.  Write down the worries that burden your mind.  Take time to ponder and respond:

Have I noticed when I am focused on praising God, my worries are crowded out? _____

_____

_____

_____

_____

_____

_____

_____

What have I wasted time worrying over recently or in the past? _____

_____

_____

_____

_____

Have I done all I need to do in these troubling situations? _____

_____

_____

_____

In my room for gratitude, what am I grateful for? _____

_____

_____

_____

_____

Where might I find partners to share gratitude? _____

_____

_____

_____

_____

Where might I find humor to use as balm for my worries and wounds? _____

_____

_____

_____

_____

Dear GOD,

It is SUMMERTIME, a time for growth & GRACE <u>after</u> repentance & RELEASE.  This is true for myself and everyone.  YES, everyone!!  As your Prophet, I see how you help us grow <u>after</u> we lay down our burdens <u>and</u> sins—things covered up, omissions, or the absence of important information.  YOU see <u>all</u> our burdens.  YOU see <u>all</u> sin.

I claim your promise in II Chronicles 7:14…

> *If my people, who are called by my name, will humble themselves and pray and seek my face and turn from their wicked ways, then will I hear from heaven and will forgive their sin and will heal their land.*

Repentance fertilizes growth and stimulates GRACE.  This <u>is</u> our new beginning!  We could stay down, cry wolf, and complain.  It seems easier to stay down than to get up and stand on your promises, to grow in your GRACE.

HOWEVER… at our weekly prayer meeting YOU called us to GET UP, be victorious, praise the name of Jesus, stop complaining.  And, we did!  WOW!  We were in need of your presence, your healing, and YOU WERE THERE!

WE SPOKE THE NAME OF JESUS and received your lifeline.
WE SPOKE THE NAME OF JESUS in love, in tenderness, and in weakness.  Brokenness melted away.
WE SPOKE THE NAME OF JESUS; gloom and pain disappeared.
WE SPOKE THE NAME OF JESUS and you washed us clean.
WE SPOKE THE NAME OF JESUS and experienced your power, presence, and healing.

WOW! As one prayer partner put it,

**"This is better than Valium!"**

LORD, we do get weary, but we learned… that it takes very little energy to repeat the name of Jesus. We learned… to rest in you and let the gentle wave of SHALOM (wholeness) roll over us. We repented, released, and experienced growth and GRACE.

We will meet you there again, LORD! We KNOW you will never let us down as we repent and praise the name of Jesus, our LORD and SAVIOR.

In Joy & Shalom,

*Sharon*

**ACTION REFLECTION:**

God knew I needed five smooth stones and sent four of us to pray together. God made up the fifth prayer partner! "Goliath" was dealt a serious blow! This prayer was "Jesus with skin on." God's presence is REAL when two or more come together in prayer. Discovering the presence of God can be so simple. For many persons, God's presence seems unattainable. Those are difficult times.

What is separating me from God's presence? _____

_____

_____

_____

_____

_____

_____

How do I know I am one of God's people? _____

_____

_____

_____

_____

With which persons do I feel closer to God? _____

_____

_____

_____

_____

_____

_____

In the name of Jesus, I can _____

_____

_____

_____

_____

_____

God, who would be willing to be my prayer partners?

_____

_____

_____

_____

_____

_____

_____

Dear GOD,

I call you GOD because you are FIRST in my life and in my death. When I walk through each day, I want YOU beside me, all around me, like a sweet cloud... leading me YOUR WAY. Each day is precious. Many things and persons snatch at, nip at, claw at me, trying to diminish the preciousness of this day. I take time to: <u>Listen</u> to the crickets, <u>hear</u> the birds outside the window, <u>notice</u> the school bus waiting for children (precious cargo in a chaotic world), <u>offer</u> a prayer on behalf of children I've never met, <u>scan</u> the newspaper (blocking ridicule from my mind) with caring and compassion for this city, state, nation, and world.

Slowing down is the ONLY way to absorb the precious, the priceless, the GOOD that YOU have encapsulated within each day, each hour, and each moment. As I do this, I pause to savor the aroma and flavor of LIFE. No one can take this from me unless I allow it. You set us free from various types of bondage through reflective moments, if not in reality, in our minds, of distant places, people, things. We are free to drift away with YOU. The timing may have to be <u>after</u> others are asleep OR <u>before</u> others are awake in the morning. Once plugged into this SOUL-MOMENT, it becomes food for the SOUL. No wonder our souls are weary, weak, dying.

Human inventions prod us into activity and away from stillness with you. Throughout the centuries you have said: BE STILL and KNOW GOD. Our living hell is created via separation from you and intrusions into stillness with you. Speak to me, LORD, in the still of the moment...

***Let's not ruin it with a lot of words, more noise, Sharon.
Let's just sit here together in quiet. I treasure these
times when <u>you</u> have time for me... ONENESS.***

102

Thank you, Lord, for allowing me to fall deeper in love with you in the stillness. I <u>pray</u> others will be able to find space for stillness, a bit of SHALOM, ONENESS, each day. Thank you for allowing moments of SHALOM from which to fill my empty vessel. Help me, LORD, to bring you other empty vessels.

Shalom,

**Sharon**

## ACTION REFLECTION:

The hectic modern lifestyle is not always our friend. Slow down!

Right now at this very moment when I listen, I hear _____
_____
_____
_____
_____
_____

When have I taken time lately to just sit with God? _____
_____
_____
_____
_____
_____
_____

I hear God in the following ways _____

_____

_____

_____

_____

_____

What have I learned that I am able to pass on? _____

_____

_____

_____

_____

_____

_____

_____

_____

How can I make a difference? _____

_____

_____

_____

_____

_____

How do I show that I care?_____

_____

_____

_____

_____

Dear GOD,

I've been reading your Book of Nehemiah, Chapter 8. After all, we are called the Nehemiah Community of Shalom. I love the part in Verse 10 where the governor, Nehemiah, says to the people:

*Go and enjoy choice food and sweet drinks, and send some to those who have nothing prepared. This day is sacred to our LORD. Do not grieve, for the joy of the LORD is your strength.*

Every day is sacred, LORD! Every day is a day to enjoy, rather than to grumble and curse. (Please forgive us!) Every day is a day to explore…

to discover "new" all around us.
to try on a child's eyes and ears.

Last evening my grandkids came to visit. They were busy "little persons" (not small adults) eagerly exploring everything in sight and within hearing. The clock chimed on the hour. "What's that, Grandma?" asked Brandon, "What's that?"

We explored and explored! Fragile houseplants were placed out of reach. Two Christmas Cactus buds were picked, placed in water where the two inquisitive ones (Brandon talking, Samantha touching) returned often to ask, "Why aren't the buds open? When will they open, Grandma?"

My squiggly, constantly-in-motion, budding persons left behind a trail of joy... fingerprints of joy... trails of unabashed exploration of all that holds wonder in their world... they see with joy... in joy. They have not yet had all the joy squashed out of them. They have not yet lost God's wholeness, that inner state of joy, SHALOM. They don't dwell on the past, yet, or worry about or fear the future. Thank you for their visit and my renewed joy in each moment. Fan into flame the dying embers of joy. Observing our JOY in daily life with Jesus... must be the best of all THANKSGIVINGS.

## *Right!*

Shalom,

*Sharon*

## ACTION REFLECTION:

The visit from my grandchildren was a blessing in the midst of my struggle to make sense of my loved one being forcibly removed from my life. I did not clean off **one set** of fingerprints on my sliding glass door. That set of fingerprints was a reminder of their precious visit. It was a holy visit.

Have I had a holy visit lately or in the past?_____
_____
_____
_____
_____

How has a child blessed my life? _____
_____

My special place of shalom (peace) is_____

I have held back the joy of young children by _____

What or who gives me the greatest joy? _____

Dear GOD,

I wander through the memories of this year. I ponder the days, the nights, the events in which I was (still am and always will be) blessed with your presence, your gift of Jesus Christ, your gift of life. THANK YOU!

There were quiet days. I absorbed your soul food.
There were full days. I saw you in many faces and places.
There were chaotic days. I called on you continually or ran from you.
There were unpleasant days. I asked you, "Why?"
There were sleepless nights. I praised your name to pass the hours.
There were nights when I awoke and you whispered, *"Rest my child."*
There were days and nights when I said, "I can't do this!"
    And you said, *"I will show you how."*
There were sad, disappointing nights, and you said, *"Joy cometh in the morning!"*

## AND YOU WERE RIGHT!

God, I did not realize how much until this moment that YOU fill my days and my nights. You make me whole (SHALOM—God's Wholeness!). I learned this from the innocent faces of a children's choir, who were singing a "Thank You" to me for speaking to them about the mission work at our church. Every face became absolutely sincere. Every set of eyes became round and pure. Angelic voices proclaimed the words:

*Thank you Lord for saving my soul.*
*Thank you Lord for making me whole.*

THANK YOU, GOD. Prepare more hearts to receive your love, your Christ Child. Let us sing your praise every day. Open us up to receive SHALOM—YOUR WHOLENESS in all areas of our lives. THANK YOU, GOD, for sending the Christ Child into a world desperately in need of him. Help all those who do not see him to recognize his presence.

THANK YOU,

*Sharon*


## ACTION REFLECTION:

Our second "prison" Christmas was approaching. Regardless of how thankful I felt at the time of writing the column, these were times when I did not think I could stand the injustice of Daniel's incarceration one more day. He was in danger. Daniel was beaten up by his "cellie," who was not mentally stable in the lockdown environment of a two-man cell.

The above issue of the church newsletter was printed on "Christmas green" paper. When photocopied, the page emerged very dark with light space around each letter. Neat… darkness surrounded by the light of Christ! All darkness is in need of Christ's light. Even in the dark of injustice, God was there. If you feel surrounded by darkness, hold on. God ventures into the darkness and ministers to us.

What darkness have I been surrounded by? _____
_____
_____
_____
_____
_____
_____

One thing I wish I could put to rest is _____
_____
_____
_____
_____

Thank you God for _____
_____
_____
_____
_____
_____

Prepare my heart to expect the *light* around the dark spaces.  I can help by _____
_____
_____
_____
_____

How am I willing to take a stand for justice wherever injustice is found? _____
_____
_____
_____
_____
_____
_____
_____

Dear GOD,

I cannot get my friend's question out of my mind. "What do you want for Christmas?" I <u>did</u> <u>not</u> <u>get</u> what I wanted for Christmas… **"PEACE ON EARTH!"**
Or, so I thought!

God, this brand new, clean, pure year is a wonderful gift, undeserved, as is your **GRACE.** I do not want to spend this year (or rather, waste it) asking, "Why?" or "When?" I want to be deserving of the love and trust YOU have given me.
You call me to be a peacemaker.
    You call us to lay down our weapons.
        You call us to cease unnecessary conflict.

### *Enough already!  Peace, <u>be</u> <u>still</u>!*
### *Love ME with all of your heart and strength and mind!*
### *AND, Love your neighbor as yourself!*

**I know, God, I know!**

### *My answers do not come according to your timing!*

**I know, God, I know!**

But God, I want to serve you and do all I can for you.  I don't know how much time I have left.  Is there something YOU want me to do?

# Just love me.

I see. I hear you. And that means???

### Focus on ME, not on your disappointments.
### Focus on ME, not on the confusion around you.
### Focus on ME and just love ME.

*"For there is still a vision for the appointed time;
it speaks of the end, and does not lie.
If it seems to tarry, wait for it;
it will surely come, it will not delay."* [Habakkuk 2:3 NRSV]

Okay, God, I will need your help to stay in focus. Get me through <u>one</u> day at a time. And, I hereby declare this month **"Just Love God"** month. Thank you for the peace in my heart.

Peace,

*Sharon*

## ACTION REFLECTION:

With many months behind us and only four months until Daniel's release date, I found it difficult to have patience. Even though I *wanted* to focus on God, it was extremely difficult. A.W. Tozer said, "The desire to fulfill the purpose for which we were created is a gift from God." My experience is… God starts with where we are and brings us to where we need to be. God was bringing me to where I needed to be. Now it's your turn…

What do I want more than anything? _____
_____
_____
_____
_____
_____

What am I willing to do for it? _____
_____
_____
_____
_____

What am I willing to give up for it? _____
_____
_____
_____

Am I sure I really want it? _____
_____
_____
_____

What does God want?  For me?  For others? _____
_____
_____
_____
_____
_____

Dear GOD,

I t is Spring! And **"O, the joy that floods my soul!"** [*Hymn, "He Touched Me"*] New life, new hope, new love, new joy—all surge up in Holy energy! The author of Ecclesiastes writes, *"There is a time for everything, and a season for every activity under heaven...."*

You have placed me here for my light to shine for a season! Now you are calling me to a season of writing. I must follow. YOU are my light, my life, and my teacher.

For three years, you have taught me, shown me your presence in the inner city on 13th Street (otherwise known as "Crack Alley"). You are present throughout the 70 square block area of the Nehemiah Community of Shalom.

You have taught me that life without YOU is meaningless and self-centered. YOU have taught me so much! Take it, LORD...

> *YES, and I AM Spirit. I AM not bricks and mortar, wood and aluminum siding. I AM not to be caged in small spaces or institutions. I AM free and need to roam, to enter persons and homes, to roam through streets and alleys, to move among crowds and beside the one sitting alone by the lakeshore, or walking in the park. I AM that which started this world. I care about this world and the entire universe! I AM the unimaginable! And yet, humans put me in chairs, on thrones, and especially in places where they want me. Often it is not too close to their personal matters.*

*I love to watch my humans, to watch them grow and laugh and find joy in this life. Just wait until you see the wonders in store for the next stage in life. If you think this is something, you have a wonderful surprise coming in due season!*

Thank you, LORD! **I know… that I know… that I know…** you are with us. Let those who do not yet see, <u>see</u> Jesus.

> We cannot <u>know</u> him without <u>seeing</u> him.
> We cannot <u>love</u> him without <u>knowing</u> him.
> We cannot <u>serve</u> him without <u>loving</u> him. [*Holy Land Lecture, Dr. Charles Page*]

I love you LORD, and Oh, what joy floods my soul!     SHALOM!!!

*Sharon*


## ACTION REFLECTION:

There was sadness in my soul because this was the last column I would write for my parish. It was time to move on. Daniel was released. We worshipped together the last Sunday I preached in the parish. I left with all things in order to begin a two-week vacation. Technically, I was still appointed to serve the parish. Three days into my vacation, the phone rang. God had another plan. Florence was dying. We had spent many hours together during her suffering. She had touched my life. I was allowed to have a sacred "Good-bye" and to officiate at her funeral. It was time to let her go.

God was present. It is a blessed assurance to know GOD IS, not was, not will be. God repeatedly says, "I AM." It is a blessed assurance to know Jesus is also present, not was, not will be. Jesus IS. Florence knew that. She was ready.

The one thing I wish I knew more fully is _____

_____

_____

_____

Where have I found God in unlikely places and situations? _____

_____

_____

_____

_____

_____

Where can I establish and nurture God's Shalom? _____

_____

_____

_____

If I were to write to God, what would I say? _____

_____

_____

_____

If God were to write me, what would God say? _____

_____

_____

_____

_____

_____

Dear GOD,

THANK YOU for one last gift! Your divine timing allowed me to be with Florence the day she died. For three years, I visited her as she faded from life to death. It was a beautiful spring day—brilliant blue sky! Out of the wind, the sunshine was warm! I was enjoying a day with Brandon, my five-year-old grandson! Florence's niece called, "Aunt Florence is dying." I responded, "I'll be right there!"

Then I realized I was faced with a dilemma. What was I to do with Brandon while Grandma completed her work in the parish? With the family's permission, I took him with me. Brandon played in the sunny backyard while I went inside to say, "Good-bye" and to pray with Florence. A large loving family was gathered around Florence in the living room, long since converted into a hospice room.

I knelt to pray softly near her ear. As I prayed aloud, I heard sniffles and weeping. There was so much love in that room. It was sad, but it was *time*. Florence had been frail for such a long time. Together, we ended with the Lord's Prayer. Then, it was quiet…

Still on my knees at her side, I heard the back door slowly squeak open. Someone entered… and came into Florence's room. The grown-ups parted and let a very determined child go to his grandma. With tears in my eyes, I looked up and received a dandelion from a chubby hand. "For her." Mistakenly, I thought he was bringing the flower to me. No, it was "for her."

It was a **Holy Moment**, a child bringing a dying woman a gift—a first fruit of spring—a symbol of new life after the winter season. Someday, Brandon and I will talk about the experience again, in more depth.

Florence's funeral was my last service in the parish. To spend that sacred time with her family was indeed a gift!  It was a chance to say a Holy "Good-bye."  And God, THANK YOU for the angels.  I know YOU will take it from here…

SHALOM,

*Sharon*


**ACTION REFLECTION:**

It was Florence's daughter, Florence Marie, who saw the angel standing behind me in the pulpit on Sunday morning.  Florence Marie is a solid, stable as they come, spiritual woman.  Her angel strengthened me when I felt I could stand no more!  Look around you.  Focus on the good and the light; you will find your way.  Ask yourself… who and what strengthens me?  Is there more good than evil present?  Is there more light than darkness?  Below is a template for you to continue the daily practice of conversations with God.  Bless you on your journey.  Converse with God who awaits…

Dear God,
    Today, I…
I thank you for…
Speak to me concerning…
I felt your presence when…
Please send me a mentor who will help me grow spiritually.

## ONE ENDING—ANOTHER BEGINNING

Remember the inflatable toy I described in the beginning? What I referred to as a "punch toy" is now called a "Bop Bag" which sells for five dollars. I purchased two "Bop Bags" for Christmas, one for Brandon, and one for Samantha. Regardless of what the toy is named, it mimics the ups and downs in life. Through these ups and downs I have grown closer to God. I've grown stronger in faith, in courage, hope, love, and peace. I've gained stability. The "bop toy" doesn't lean all the way to the floor anymore when I take an emotional or spiritual punch. I am grateful for the healing process of writing this book. I could not have done it without God's help or without these experiences. *Stand With Angels,* even though it is not the Christian testimony I would have chosen, is a gift I accept with joy and peace.

## SPIRITUAL MENTORS

I could not have grown without spiritual mentors. In hindsight, it was much easier to see the effects of numerous persons. This is not an exhaustive list, nor is it in any particular order. Some of these persons did not even realize they were my mentors. Also, spiritual growth was not painless or effortless. In the beginning, I mentioned we all have crises. A spiritual crisis hit me with a whole mountain of pain 30 years ago when my two-and-a-half year old son was killed in an automobile accident. My best friend was driving. She and her unborn child died also. The following summer our baby was stillborn. In less than one year, my husband and I stood beside the graves of two wee sons. Our hearts were broken. We read about these things in the newspaper. We never really think it will happen to *us*. We asked every question imaginable.

It is a heartbreaking experience to bury your children. It changes you forever. I needed *different* answers. I could not believe *"It was God's will"* that children are crushed in cars so God can have children in his flower garden. I needed them in my flower garden. What kind of God hurls cars into bridges in order to snatch children away? Not my God!

My search lasted several years. Faithfully, I attended a Tuesday morning Bible Study. I asked zillions of questions. I found *different* answers… other than the ones well-intentioned people gave me at the funerals. Sometimes I wonder if my two tiny sons were supernatural mentors helping me through this painful process. My empty arms kept me determined to learn, grow, and heal spiritually.

My pastor, Rev. Peabody, a second career person retired from farming, was a spiritual mentor. Both he and his wife, Mary Ellen, listened and allowed me to find my way through the difficult questions. I remember vividly the day I read Romans 8:28 and claimed it for my own. **"We know that all things work together for good for those who love God, who are called according to his purpose."** [*NRSV*] God did not cause the accident, but God was able to bring good out of tragedy. Light was forming at the end of the tunnel!

Our small group met week after week. In this Bible study group, my flickering faith was fanned into flame. When God put the pieces of my broken heart back together, I was on fire! *I knew… that I knew… that I knew…* God was alive. My sons were alive in God's love and I would be okay. I would survive this experience and be even stronger than before.

As we worked our way through the Bible, the name Corrie ten Boom kept coming up. I read her books: The Hiding Place, A Prisoner And Yet…, Tramp For the Lord. If Corrie ten Boom could survive what she survived as a result of the Nazi invasion, I could survive my losses. Her life story changed my life. Corrie was in her mid-seventies when I first came to know her through her books and movie "The Hiding Place." I was both sad and joyful when she died in her nineties, still traveling and preaching for the Lord. If an innocent person could be imprisoned unjustly, and emerge years later to tell the miracles and the faith story with love and grace, maybe, just maybe… I could also!

Corrie was a spiritual mentor. Through Corrie and her sister (who died in prison) I learned of Psalm 100. I learned to enter God's presence with praise and thanksgiving, regardless of what I was going through. This psalm has served me well, even when I did not feel like offering praise and thanksgiving to God or anybody. This psalm has served me well by coming into God's presence by singing. One

Sunday morning shortly after Daniel was accused, I turned to the organist and said, "I <u>need</u> to sing!" From that Sunday on, we sang our favorite hymns and choruses before the service began. Someone said, "The worship has already begun!" The simple acts of finding something to be thankful for and of singing had a transforming effect on my spirit. God used Corrie ten Boom to help me find my courage. Corrie helped me rise above my fears and take a stand for justice in unjust situations. I believe angels stand with me. After our wedding, my daughters gave Daniel and I a gift certificate for a massage. Unknown to them, the massage therapist was a devout Jew who prayed for her clients *as* she massaged. She was skilled in Reiki and had the ability to see angels during her massage sessions. After Daniel's massage, she said, "There were angels everywhere! Daniel was surrounded by angels!"

Isn't it interesting how simply telling our story as Corrie did (it used be called giving your testimony) has power to inspire others? Isn't it interesting that the one who inspired me most in the 20th Century was held prisoner? She served time; she was one of the outcasts. Decades later, I realized I was in love with two convicted criminals, Daniel and Jesus. Jesus was never exonerated in any court of law. He stood and now we stand with the outcasts, the incarcerated. We never thought it would happen to us! It has become an honor, a privilege! We have gained more than we lost.

Some spiritual mentors were people I never met personally. After my call to ministry, I remember watching Dr. Schuller's "Hour of Power" and hearing the reading of Jeremiah 29:11, **"For I know the plans I have for you," declares the LORD, "plans to prosper you and not to harm you, plans to give you hope and a future."** It was as if God personally spoke those words to *me*. Another time, as I was going through the death of my first marriage, I heard Dr. Schuller say, "In love's service <u>only</u> broken hearts qualify." His positive thinking and preaching made an impact on me. The guests who shared testimonies of what they had survived with God's help made an impact on me. Again, I became aware of the power within each of our faith-journeys and how our story can help others. *Telling the story turns evil on its head!*

Years ago, I read Dr. Schuller's book: <u>The Be-Happy Attitudes</u>. This year, I read it again. The first time I read his book it did not speak to me as it did now! Of all the things people have said to us or I have read during this time of personal tribulation, none were as comforting as Dr. Schuller's book on the Beatitudes. Nothing was as comforting as the famous lines from Jesus' "Sermon on the Mount":

Blessed are the poor in spirit, for theirs is the kingdom of heaven.
Blessed are those who mourn, for they shall be comforted.
Blessed are the meek, for they shall inherit the earth.
Blessed are those who hunger and thirst for righteousness, for they shall be satisfied.
Blessed are the merciful, for they shall obtain mercy.
Blessed are the pure in heart, for they shall see God.
Blessed are the peacemakers, for they shall be called children of God.
Blessed are those who are persecuted for righteousness' sake, for theirs is the kingdom of heaven.

And this line, which was *not* part of his book, was especially comforting: "Blessed are you when people insult you, persecute you and falsely say all kinds of evil against you because of me." Daniel and I could write a whole book on the verse Dr. Schuller didn't write about.

Recently these same Beatitudes were the topic of Bishop Sharon Brown Christopher's message to the newly ordained ministers and members of the annual conference (the conference covers two-thirds of the state of Illinois). Bishop Christopher said, "You are doing something right… when you *are* the Beatitudes." My head nodded "Yes!" throughout her message. Our troubles do not always come be-cause we did something wrong. Sometimes our troubles come because we are doing something *right…* and others do not like it!

My ordination class traveled with Bishop Christopher to the Holy Land. As we shared our first supper in Galilee, Bishop Christopher was willing to *listen* and to *hear* my cry for justice. She has become a spiritual mentor. Her column is filled with truth and justice. She speaks with a voice that reaches the practical side of our lives and encourages us to trust all that is *holy*. She encourages us to become as a child, to stand with the impoverished because that is *where* we find Jesus. I have experi-enced Christ's presence as I stand with the powerless, the poor, the outcasts.

Rev. Alice Shirley is another of my mentors. Her modern day parable using the "Little Jessica" story gave me courage and inspiration hundreds of times. Rev. Shirley sat with us through the trial, through the sentencing, through every situation. She also officiated at our wedding after Daniel was released from prison. Alice was right. We don't realize what God is doing, but God is doing something. We could not fully understand the image until we caught a glimpse of the activity above us, working to secure **something far better** for us than being trapped deep down in a well of injustice. Little Jessica was our "hope" image. We needed hope! God used Alice to help me be more than I ever thought I could be. Watch for those persons who inspire you to be the person God created you to be.

Several famous persons who I have never met have inspired me. Oprah Winfrey is one of those persons. I first encountered Oprah playing the part of "Sofia" in the movie "Color Purple." I remember leaving the theater feeling depressed. There was something about the movie that touched the very core of my being. The injustices, the travesty of young girls being violated, the letters Celie wrote to God, all touched me in a very personal way. For years, I watched Oprah on TV. On a daily basis Oprah's show would address numerous difficult topics and causes. I admired her from a distance. She was making a difference in this world. She was standing with angels and taking a stand for justice wherever injustice was found <u>long</u> before I started wearing a yellow ribbon with an angel pin on top. The ribbon-angel pin was my symbol of taking a stand for justice. Perhaps Oprah has a similar longing to make a difference. I have a deep longing to make a difference, to leave this world a better place than I found it.

Recently, I heard Oprah explain the "Grateful Journals." She said we should buy three journals, one for ourselves, two to give away. Her philosophy of *passing on good things* is part of my philosophy. I challenge you to buy two copies of **Stand With Angels**; give one away. Or, buy a copy of another book that has been meaningful to you and share it with someone. There would not be the degree of evil in our world if we would only pass on to two other persons the GOOD STUFF of life we have received. God does not expect us to keep it to ourselves. GOOD was meant to be shared. The bad stuff gets multiplied far too much. We can help counteract bad stuff by passing on good stuff! I use the word STUFF a lot. I have a very practical down-to-earth side. *Stuff* works for me.

Bill Cosby is another famous person who has inspired me. Years ago, I learned of his millions of dollars of philanthropy toward the education of students. If God has blessed you with millions, give some of it away! You can't outgive God! And, of course, the Cosby family knows the pain of losing a son. Their pain touches my pain. Long before that, I learned from Bill Cosby the philosophy of giving back. He has received, but he doesn't keep it all to himself. We need to give back to others. This is my time of giving back. Kenneth Lay (who has a Ph.D. in Economics) once said, "You make a *living* by what you get. You make a *life* from what you give." I believe that statement should apply to more than our finances. We are able to make a difference in our world by giving to others wisdom we have learned on our journey. As well, we are able to model and emulate love, faith, hope, and peace to our families, children, grandchildren, and others.

Martha Williamson and the cast of "Touched By An Angel" have inspired me. From my living room television set, I saw a healthy, simple holistic theology that people of the 20th and 21st Centuries have been seeking. **God is love.** The only thing I hate is what evil does to people. That is all the room I have for hate in my life. I am too busy loving people to make time to hate. God does not take away all of my pain, or all of my problems. However, God does not abandon me either. I just cannot always see the presence of God or the presence of angels in supernatural form or in human form. I can seek mentors such as Roma Downey, who plays Monica. For example, Ms. Downey seeks harmony both on and off the set. I can learn to pay attention to who and what brings harmony to my life. I can learn to pay attention to what brings chaos. These observations help me make wiser choices.

I do not have to see everything at all times. It would probably confuse me even more in my limited human mind, emotions, and body. I remind you—I did not see the angel standing behind me. I have never to my knowledge seen a supernatural angel. However, I believe in God. I believe in angels. I do not have to see it all! I merely need enough faith and hope and love to get me through one more day.

Mentors from all walks of life help me achieve my daily task. God speaks to me from the pages of a book, from the television set, sometimes a movie, sometimes the "still, small inner voice," sometimes through one of my daughters, a neighbor, or a friend. I believe in and treasure the HOLY BIBLE. I do not believe God is restricted to one book alone, but uses many ways to reach out to humanity. God does not have limitations. I have limitations! I have invisible barriers, which need to come down. I need to be open to God's leading, to God's reaching out to me. Mentors help this process.

There were, of course, mentors from seminary. I claim as a mentor Dr. Ruth Duck, a woman who has edited and written numerous books full of beautiful inclusive liturgy. Her books have inspired women all over the world (as well as men). Two months before entering seminary, I attended an international Clergywomen's Convocation. I entered the opening session as Ruth was introduced and asked to stand. Several thousand women greeted her with a standing ovation. On campus, Ruth lived in the apartment below mine. Every time I bought one of her books, I was at her door asking her to autograph it. Her classes, books, and words were liberating and healing.

And there was Dr. Robert Tuttle, who used to say to his class, "Sweet as I am, not everybody likes me." We would chuckle. In ministry, there will always be someone in your parish who has decided they don't like you or your style or whatever! In life, the workplace, at home, there will always be someone who doesn't like you! Dr. Tuttle used to say, *"I know… that I know… that I know…,"* a statement I had been saying years before I met him. In his class on "Theology of the Holy Spirit", we shared prayer and the laying on of hands for healing. I left class that day with a physical healing in my back. Today, I carry a photo clipped to my daily calendar of a woman who laid hands on the painful area of my back. I carry the photo to remind myself never to forget—miracles <u>do</u> happen! Bob Tuttle believes in miracles, in healing. He was a spiritual mentor.

Many people touch our lives. We, in turn, touch them, bless them. Life has a way of going in circles. My district superintendent imagines circles going in an upward spiral, moving closer to the holy, closer to God. So, in full circle of the upward spiral, I returned to my seminary to attend the graduation ceremony of Tom, "best man" at our wedding. I describe Tom as being more like Jesus than any person I know. He has the bluest eyes (<u>if</u> Jesus' eyes were blue, they would be <u>this</u> <u>blue</u>). He is in his late twenties, early thirties. He has a sweet spirit. He seems to appear out of nowhere! For example, he just *appeared* at the airport before we left for the Holy Land. Or the phone rings, and there he is!

As I watched Tom graduate, I thought of all that had happened since my graduation four years ago. It seemed more like <u>ten</u> years than four! I said to my friend Judy, "We were thrown to the wolves!" We left seminary for full-time ministry and were literally thrown to the wolves! I recalled Jesus' words to the 72 disciples: **"Go! I am sending you out like lambs among wolves."** [*Luke 10:3*]

One of the speakers at Tom's graduation reminded us through a story that took place in a restaurant—our cup has to be turned *over* to be filled (with coffee). Our cup has to be turned over to be filled with God's Spirit. And, it is *as* we turn evil on its head by sharing our survival story to the world that we are filled again and again. Such was the case for Corrie ten Boom. By telling her story of God's love in the midst of Ravensbruck, she turned evil on its head. Our cup becomes Jesus' cup. We become able to "drink (from) his cup and be baptized with his baptism." [*Mark 10:38, 39*] We drink from the cup of pain and suffering and survive the baptism of fire. Jesus becomes part of us; we are part of him.

Many times, Tom would send a card or letter with Romans 8:38, 39 next to his signature. Each time, I would look it up in my Bible:

> **For I am convinced that neither death nor life, neither angels nor demons, neither the present nor the future, nor any powers, neither height nor depth, nor anything else in all creation, will be able to separate us from the love of God that is in Christ Jesus our Lord.**

Tom was right! *Nothing* could separate us from the *love* of God. Mentors come in all sizes, shapes, ages, and all walks of life. Who are your mentors? These are a few of mine. God will send you mentors. Just ASK**!**
And ASK! And ASK!
And ASK!

## LEARNING EXPERIENCES FOR SHARON & DANIEL

This experience has changed Daniel's life forever. It has changed my life forever. We have experienced a humbleness we had not anticipated. No one enjoys being leveled. No one enjoys being knocked down, beaten up, or lied about. When you live with the incarcerated, you see a different side of life, life from the underside. Yes, we are changed; we are different.

The correctional officers noticed the *difference*. One officer asked Daniel, "Can I ask you a question? What in the ____ are *you* doing in here?" It's **okay** to be different!

Prior to these trials and tribulations, we never thought much about the incarcerated. As we gave our testimony to The Full Gospel Business Men's Fellowship, Daniel stated: "If you're running under the illusion that everybody in prison is there because he/she deserves it, please lose that thought! Six per cent just lose their case." Prior to this, we did not know statistically—six per cent are innocent. Some, like us, just lose their case. Some plea bargain because they are afraid of getting a longer sentence. Many, without money, have no options. We never thought about a trial being unfair or a witness being tainted. We never thought about news reports being inaccurate or biased. We never realized what damage half-truths in the media could do. We never asked, "Who submitted this information and with what motive?" We never asked, "How accurate is this article?"

We never really cared about ex-cons. We were part of the luxurious middle to upper class who did not believe it could happen to them. It happened to Jesus... and He was, He is, the best of the best! We did not know these things. Our African American friends and ethnic minority friends *know* these things. We did not want to learn these lessons. We have learned humility. This humility is not the usual type of humility! It has become *humility with enthusiasm* in telling the story of *GOD WITH US*.

God was with us the day Daniel was released. I drove to the correctional facility to pick him up. I brought him home to call his parole agent and to await further instructions. We sat at the kitchen table... looking at each other... in silence. We had a cup of coffee in a room filled with *God's presence.* How precious it was to sit at a table with someone you love in the absence of prison walls and guards!

We grew, and growth is painful! People talk about being "rooted in faith." Our roots grew, and we sprouted branches. God did not reject us; we were pulled in like a magnet. God did not rejoice; God wept with us. And, now we are present with:

...John & Luella, also falsely accused;
...Ed & Teresa, whose son may be going to Federal Prison soon;
...Danny, who plea bargained to something he <u>didn't do</u> because he was threatened with getting more time for a burglary he <u>did do</u> in a moment of stupidity;
...Michael, who Daniel helped get his GED and culinary arts degree while in prison. Michael now has a future after prison instead of going back to selling drugs;
...Julio, the gang leader who saved Daniel from serious bodily harm at the hands of his gang. Julio feared going back to his old neighborhood, being sucked back into crime, and sent back to prison. The outcasts have names and faces now. We cannot act as if we don't see or know their faces.

Through these trials, God has taught us *who we are* and *what we are* about. We are about triumph over evil. We are about rebounding after setbacks; we are about getting up after going down. We are about taking *one more step* in faith and letting go of fear. We are about loving each other as Jesus showed us how and as he loves us. We are about taking stands for justice wherever injustice is found. We are about building bridges of peace and melting barriers to God's love. We are about pursuing a journey with God that is never dull, never boring! We are about the process of being purified and of learning wisdom on the way. We are about learning the hazards on the trail as we avoid some of the wolves and pitfalls. We are about picking one another up, those who are torn by the wolves. We are about pulling others out who have fallen into the pits. As we go through trials, we learn some things cannot be avoided. Our children learn through falling and bumping their heads. So do we!

Serving the inner city was a good place to be during the personal injustice Daniel and I were experiencing. The people of the Shalom Zone understood injustice. They lived surrounded by injustice. They were courageous persons. You learn courage when you need it. You learn justice when you need release from injustice. No pain, no gain. WE GAINED. We are gaining new insights daily in how *God was there* through angels!

| **Angels ministered to me…** | **Daniel's Angels…** |
|---|---|
| Florence Marie's angel | Harvey, and Glenn |
| Jane, an angel | Jacob, Steve, Dan, Scott |
| Milton, an angel | John, Dr. Stein, Diane and Bob |
| My daughters, angels | Bruce and Joyce, Kent, Julio |
| Friends, angels | FGBMFI, Bill and Imogene, John and |
| Carol, Cindy, Florence | Ginny, Vince and Kathy, Bob and Camille |

I know I am forgetting some of our angels. God doesn't forget! I will never forget my support group, which grew silently as time passed: Al, Joyce, Norma, Lynda, Pat, Becky and Bob, GayeEllen, Ron and Doris, Bob and Felicia, Jack and Jean, Wallie and Debbie, Jane, Rita, Ken, Roy and Kay, the Volunteers In Mission. In hindsight, the list goes on and on. At the time, we felt abandoned. In Matthew 4:11 when Jesus came out of the wilderness, it says, **"Then the devil left him, and angels came and attended him."** We didn't always see or sense the presence of angels until we were coming out of our wilderness. In Mark 1:13 it says Jesus was **"in the desert forty days, being tempted by Satan. He was with the wild animals, and angels attended him."**. We *know* the wild animals, but we also know the angels.

It was Monday. I met with four other pastors, part of a support group for urban ministry in the office of our District Superintendent. The Superintendent had to leave for another meeting. As we were about to leave, I said to them, "I would like for you to pray with me. The trial begins next Monday." They sat there, squirmed in their chairs, and ignored my request. I waited and thought, "They're not going to pray. They're not going to get away with this." I said, "I asked for prayer. This situation is serious!" I heard one excuse after another. No one offered to pray. I left. Tears filled my eyes as I reached the door. As I got into my car, tears washed down my face. The emotional pain was intense; I felt rejected by my "support group." I pulled into my garage, closed the door. I thought, "If I leave the car running, I could be out of this pain in a few hours." I sat there sobbing. Finally, I thought of my daughters. How much I loved them. I thought of my grandkids. I couldn't do this. I reached up, turned off the key, went in the house, wept for nearly two hours, dried my tears, and went on.

The Sunday following my request for prayer, I led worship and preached as usual. Sunday school followed, in which I led the young adult class. Halfway through class, Florence Marie said, "You know… while you were preaching… there was *this light* behind you. The *light* kept getting larger. Then it became really large, and I could see this *angel standing* behind you."

The entire class sat in silence. Florence was as solid a person as I have ever known. There was nothing radical or flakey about this woman! I took a deep breath. "You know, I think God wanted you to share that with me. I have had a rough week!" Florence came back with, "I didn't know that." I said, **"God did!"** It got much rougher over the next six months. Florence's angel was a mystery to me, but extremely edifying in my spirit. Her angel was the first and only visible supernatural angel.

Milton was the angel who showed up in human form. Daniel had been incarcerated for several months when a gentle, quiet man came in and sat right down front during worship. Some would not call him "normal," although he appeared to be intelligent. Many would think of him as developmentally challenged. His features were symptomatic of a person with Down's Syndrome. I did not know who he was; I had never met him before. But he seemed to be right *with me* all through the worship service.

After the service, I went to the door to shake hands as people were leaving worship. He introduced himself as Milton and said, "I have a message for you, James 1:2-12." I thought this was rather strange, but I went immediately to my office to look up the text. It begins… **"Consider it pure joy, my brothers and sisters, whenever you face trials of many kinds, because you know that the testing of your faith develops perseverance."** It ends with… **"Blessed is the one who perseveres under trial…."**

I stepped out of my office. I invited Milton to stay for the young adult class, where he told us more of his story and his reason for being in Springfield. Milton was from New Orleans. God sent him to Springfield to give a message to *someone*. He did not know who the person was… until now. The members of the class and I looked at one another. We understood. We shared with Milton the trials Daniel and I had gone through the past year. And then, he left. The last we heard from Milton was a message he left on the church answering machine with his address. He asked us to "Keep in touch!" We sent him the church newsletter for over a year… until it came back stamped: **Undelivered— Address Unknown.**

*God was there.* The day Daniel was sentenced and incarcerated, my daughter Lori rode with us to the courthouse. She is a Lieutenant in the Department of Corrections. I lovingly say, "My daughter Lori is not as delicate and sweet like me!" We refer to Lori as "Zena, Warrior Princess." Lori does not want to do what I do, and I do not want to do what she does. However, I am very proud of her because I know she is fair and she does her job well. Someone needs to do her job! When Daniel was convicted, it did a "head trip" on Lori. She believed the system worked. She was learning another side of the system.

And so, she coached Daniel for two hours on the drive to the courthouse on how to "stay alive." Lori told him things <u>not</u> to say, to say, who <u>not</u> to associate with, the ins and outs of prison existence. Arriving at the courthouse, we discovered dozens and dozens of letters had been written to the judge, but it did not matter. It was over. Nothing was going to make it all go away!

The judge pronounced the sentence of four years. He directed the bailiff to handcuff and take Daniel away. People started crowding around Daniel. I could not get near him to give him a hug and a kiss "Good-bye." I looked through the crowd and there was Lori… with tears running down her face, giving Daniel a kiss on the cheek. That was not my rough and tough Lori, who never kissed her dad or anyone in public, who never wept in public. *That was God.*

God was in Julio, the gang leader who interceded when his gang was going to beat up Daniel. Within two hours, Julio got Daniel moved to a different dorm room in the minimum security prison. What Daniel and Julio did not know until later was… the Tuesday morning prayer meeting was in full swing during this altercation. One of the women from the neighborhood lay face down, prostrate on the floor and prayed, "God, I give <u>all</u> my prayers to Daniel today. I want <u>all</u> my answers to prayer to go to him today." I remember thinking, "Oh, my, that's nice! I hope she doesn't need them."

God was in the Full Gospel Business Men's Fellowship who asked to hear my testimony. They anointed me with oil on Daniel's behalf. They prayed for his safety.

God was in John and Ginny, the first to come into the prison to sing and pray with us as a couple for the first time in 15 months. It was the first time I'd heard Daniel sing in nearly two years. One of the things I loved about him was his beautiful voice. He had the ability to sing like Pavarotti. He could also play the guitar and sing like Kenny Rogers. However, his vocal cords were injured when the paramedics were trying to save his life. Besides, it is difficult to sing when your heart and spirit are broken. I Pray God will heal his brokenheart, his spirit, and his voice!

God was in Tammy, who was sharing her testimony with the Full Gospel Business Men's Fellowship. I went to hear her story, and she sponsored me on a spiritual retreat called a "Walk to Emmaus" that was extremely healing. Tammy would say, "I get excited when new trials come my way. It makes my testimony so much more interesting!"

God was in Howard, my District Superintendent, who prayed for us after the trial and conviction. Since then, I've pondered how difficult it would be to verbalize any prayer that might minister to someone in our shoes!

God was in the CEO who believed God wanted him to offer Daniel a job (sight unseen) upon his release. He asked for a resumé. Daniel sent him one from prison. The CEO said, "I can take care of this." From all of this we learned:

**God was not** the oppressor.
**God was not** the unjust judge.
**God was not** the accuser.

## LEARNING EXPERIENCES FOR SEEKERS

You will learn if you are willing. You can learn from every obstacle, every adventure, every mistake, every wise step, every attempt at dialogue with the Divine. You can learn an active, dynamic, spiritual life. You are not alone. Others are seeking God, seeking deeper meaning in life. One's certainty in a belief system is not always found, often is not found, in a church building.

I believe people want to experience God's presence and interaction in their lives. I believe seekers are not satisfied with merely just sitting through a church service. The church foundation is vital, but people want *more*. There is a hunger for the spiritual dimension of life that religious practice alone does not fill. Once the seekers find the active, dynamic presence of God in their personal lives, they seek a place to live out their beliefs. However, I do not believe seekers want a fairytale god. I believe they want the real thing, one who cares about them when they go through tough times, one who can communicate with them (i.e., an inner voice that is more than their own personal conscience) and guide them. Why would anyone want to follow or worship a God who is absent, voiceless, or indifferent?

People of the New Millenium want MORE, and they deserve more. If the church has taught or acted out that God is absent, voiceless or indifferent, then no wonder many churches are shrinking in numbers. Make no mistake, I needed, still need, the teachings I learned in church and Sunday school. I needed, still need, Bible stories, and teachers who cared and modeled a life of faith, hope, love and peace. A great deal of the doctrine and dogma, I didn't need. However, our predecessors were struggling with their own faith journey in the midst of their own pain and crises. They didn't *always* get it right. The leaders and people of the New Millenium will not always get it right. Humans will always need to look at what others have carved out of their life experiences. Each person must forge ahead discovering that which is worthy and true and that which still relates to him/her as a person, a child of God. No one's journey is identical to another's journey. Most New Millenium seekers recognize this.

Science helps us recognize this. Science informs us of the uniqueness of each snowflake, each fingerprint, each DNA molecule. Science informs us there is something far greater outside our planet Earth and our solar system. When are we going to realize God will not fit in a box? God will not be boxed in. Life is unpredictable.

However, joy, peace, hope, love and faith are still possible. For example, I was called upon recently to do a wedding during a snow storm. My phone rang at 1:30 in the afternoon. "We have a very un-happy bride. The wedding is scheduled for 4 o'clock today, and the minister is snowed in and can't get out. Could you officiate at the service?" After a few questions, I said, "Yes, I will. I can get to the church." I prepared and drove cautiously to the church, avoiding the deeper snowdrifts. The bride arrived; she was running late. The groom arrived even later. Members of the wedding party drifted in—some of who were not expected to arrive due to the weather conditions. The guests were few but caring.

I assured the bride it was going to be a beautiful wedding. It was. To the bride and groom and all those gathered for the ceremony I said, "You will never forget this day! Years from now you will tell stories of this. You will laugh at what just a few hours ago brought tears. You will learn what you thought wasn't going to happen, can still happen. Your dreams can still come true, maybe a few hours (or years) later, but definitely possible! You can learn from this day that *no matter* what life throws at you—snow storms, interruptions, challenges, disappointments—you will get through it."

Life is a struggle. Like that couple—we face great odds and we need determination and commit-ment! The potential for JOY is still possible. It takes faith to believe obstacles can be overcome. We can learn that *with* God all things are possible.  God makes a way, opens doors.  God gives new dreams.  God touches our lives.  These mentors, these experiences, these angels have all touched my life.  I am changed.  I am renewed.  Because of that, I have a new dream, the dream of founding a "Touch of Life" center.  Far too often, a church becomes a building used to barricade the neighborhood out and a place to *protect* the presence of God from "outsiders."  Far too often, we notice differences and forget precious common bonds.  I believe these centers are a model, a paradigm, for the 21st Century inviting people to grow spiritually.

God's touch of LIFE is needed in <u>all</u> areas of our lives.  We need God's touch in our communities, in the spiritual, in the physical, in the emotional areas of our lives.  We need God's touch through support groups for young persons, young couples and new parents.  We need <u>excellent</u>, not just adequate child care centers.  Far too many people are falling through the cracks.  I believe the remedy is in supporting and nurturing young parents *as* they raise their children.  I believe far too many persons are in prison merely because they do not know how to make wise decisions or how to cope with the hazards in life.  We need ministry with the incarcerated and ex-offenders, but we need preventative methods beginning with healthy marriages and healthy ways to raise our children.

We need God's touch through grandparents who are able to mentor others.  We need God's touch in our social events, family reunions, and fund-raising events for special needs.  We need God's touch through spiritual retreats.  We need a place to worship, <u>not only</u> on Saturday evening and Sunday morning, but a Holy place to rest and be renewed any time and day of the week.  We need a place where the focus is <u>not</u> on passing the offering plate and counting those present.  We need a place where the *total focus* is on worshiping God.  When we offer something holy and helpful to people, God will make a way for tithes and donations to sustain it.  My passion and goal is to touch someone's life with God's presence.  God will do the rest.

## THE EPIPHANY

God was our Epiphany, our light. Let me explain what I mean. An Epiphany experience is one in which a manifestation of the Divine is revealed by way of some form of light. It is an unmistakable, clear way in which God shows us something we need to see or know. The origin of Epiphany dates back to the 3rd Century, when January 6 was declared the celebration of the Magi who followed the star and found the Christ Child.

May I share an Epiphany experience with you? Back in the fall of Daniel's first year of incarceration, I was visiting him at the Canton D.O.C. facility. Daniel always wanted me to stay as long as possible. I had planned to leave around 5 o'clock for the long drive home. For some unknown reason about 4 o'clock, Daniel felt a nudge and said "You need to go *now.*"

I left, drove into Canton, where I had my Dairy Queen comfort food—the "Full Meal Deal"complete with hot fudge sundae. I was finishing up the sundae when I heard someone say, "You can't see the rainbow from there." I thought, "Rainbow! I love rainbows!" I devoured the rest of the sundae and went outside, where I could see part of a double rainbow. I decided I would be able to see it much better from the highway south of Canton, and I proceeded to drive home. As I drove out of town, on my left I saw the most perfect full double rainbow I had ever seen. To complement this beauty, the setting sun was shining on the golden fall leaves moist with raindrops. I drove along, drinking in the surrealistic beauty. It was magical! It soothed my soul!

I turned west after a few miles and drove directly into the setting sun—a perfect golden ball—resting in the center of the highway. Having extremely light-sensitive eyes, my first reaction would typically have been to lower the visor and grab for my sunglasses. I did neither. The bright light felt... warm, soothing, wonderful. This not being my norm, I asked, ***"God, is this a sign?"***

Immediately, IMMEDIATELY, out of the passenger's side of the windshield, there was a billboard, a BILLBOARD... which responded to my question—"With God All Things Are Possible."

I never did put on my sunglasses.  I never lowered the visor.  I never turned on the radio.  I drove home (two hours) in the most powerful spirit-filled silence I have ever experienced.  I did not want anything to intrude upon the presence of God that filled our Ford Escort!

*If I had waited until 5 o'clock to leave for home, I would have missed the Epiphany!*

**"With God all things are possible"** is from Matthew 19:26.  It is the story Jesus told of the rich young man who asked the question, "Who then can be saved?"  Jesus was honest about life not being easy.  He tells of the largest of animals (in his land), the camel, being unable to go through the smallest of spaces, an eye of a needle.  I hear him saying, "It is humanly impossible to save ourselves, but **With God all things are possible!**  We couldn't save ourselves from going through this experience.  However, against all odds… we celebrate our marriage.  We celebrate the healing process.  We are living proof…"With God All Things Are Possible."

I believe God should have the last word…

Dear Sharon,

I AM glad I was able to help, able to be there with you and for you during those painful times. Often, I was silent. You didn't need more words. You needed my loving acceptance, my hug, my strength, my courage, my peace. I was there. I AM here.

People need to learn how simple it is to connect with ME. Frenzy and fear do not help. Only stillness and peace will help. A 31-day book is a great idea for this rushed world of humans.

Animals, plants, the stars, the sun, the moon—do not rush. They are within my harmony. Humans get out of sync. Peace, BE STILL with ME. You are MINE.

I love my children. My love is even greater than your love for your children and grandchildren. My love is flawless, unconditional, perfect. Perfect love casts out fear. Do not be bound up in fear. **Stand with angels! Stand with Jesus Christ!**

Love,
  God

*Hope looks up... and beyond.*

*Wait three days!*

*Where was God in this day?*

*God loves me. God loves you.*

# Order Form

Please fill out this form, remove it from this copy of the book, and send it with a check or money order.

Send orders To:  Angel Writing Mill
                   106 Genoa Drive
                   Suite 101
                   Springfield, IL 62703-5704

I wish to order \_\_\_\_\_ copies of *Stand With Angels*

| | |
|---|---|
| Price per book | $15.98 |
| Illinois Sales Tax on all orders | 1.16 per copy |
| Shipping and Handling | 3.20 |
| TOTAL | $20.34 per copy |

**TOTAL FOR THIS ORDER:**
_____ COPIES AT $20.34 EACH = $_____ (Please allow 2-3 weeks for processing)

- - - - - - - - - - - - - - - - - - - - - - - - - - - - - - - - - - -

Angel Writing Mill
106 Genoa Drive, Suite 101
Springfield, IL 62703-5704

           SHIP TO:

_____

_____

_____